Learning
to
Lead

Learning
to
Lead

*The Art of
Transforming
Managers
into Leaders*

Jay A. Conger

 Jossey-Bass Publishers
San Francisco

For sales outside the United States, contact Maxwell Macmillan International Publishing Group, 866 Third Avenue, New York, New York 10022.

Manufactured in the United States of America.

The paper used in this book is acid-free and meets the State of California requirements for recycled paper (50 percent recycled waste, including 10 percent postconsumer waste), which are the strictest guidelines for recycled paper currently in use in the United States.

Library of Congress Cataloging-in-Publication Data

Conger, Jay Alden.
    Learning to lead : the art of transforming managers into leaders / Jay A. Conger. — 1st. ed.
        p.   cm. — (The Jossey-Bass management series)
    Includes bibliographical references and index.
    ISBN 1-55542-474-0
    1. Leadership. I. Title. II. Series.
HD57.7.C665   1992
658.4'09—dc20   92-16934
                                                       CIP

FIRST EDITION
HB Printing   10 9 8 7 6 5 4 3 2   *Code 9272*

The Jossey-Bass
Management Series

To Ralph Biggadike, Jack Gabarro,
David Gregory, John Kotter,
Patrick Mahoney, Jeff Schaler, and Jack Weber
—teachers who have helped me learn to lead

Contents

Preface

*A*s part of their desperate search for improved competitiveness, corporations are pouring millions of dollars into some form or other of leadership training. Executives and human resource professionals commit their companies' valuable resources to such training because of the ever-pressing and serious shortage of leaders. With almost blind faith, managers cross their fingers and pin their hopes on programs that may or may not produce lasting results.

The same desperate search to develop leaders characterizes our educational system. A number of graduate business programs have initiated leadership courses and "leadership weeks" to transform their graduates into leaders *extraordinaire*. But instead of looking ahead for new methods or contexts for learning, many have turned to what training companies and corporations have been offering for the last decade: action-learning experiences and Outward Bound–type adventures. They, too, seem to be unsure how to train leaders.

Then there are the trainers and teachers, most of whom are dedicated to creating classroom experiences that will positively and profoundly affect how teachers and students alike learn about leadership. It would deeply satisfy us to find the right combination of experiential and intellectual instruction that could spark a lifetime of leadership ability in our students and seminar participants. Yet we who teach and train have also been struggling with the difficulty of finding approaches that have lasting impact.

No matter how we look at the issue, the question still is whether managers can actually be trained to become leaders. So many factors influence the effects of training that we cannot say with any precision what its real contribution is. In fact, no one has ever taken the time to seriously investigate what is offered in leadership training programs and to ascertain whether any of them work. Furthermore, leadership itself is complex, and its qualities are difficult to measure. So while the field of leadership training has assumed increasing importance in terms of both the skills society needs and the resources corporations devote to it, relatively little is known about its effectiveness. A teenager I know has a favorite saying that sums up the problem: "Looks like a big mess to me."

In *Learning to Lead* I aim to make sense of this "mess" by examining actual training programs and the results they produce. As a result, this is the first book that explores the issue of leadership training with a critical eye for what works and what does not. To do this, though, requires a bit of bravery and foolhardiness on my part—bravery because the art and science of leadership training, as mentioned, is uncharted territory; foolhardiness because I personally should know better than to explore such unknown terrain, especially topic areas so complex and difficult to research with precision, as this one is. But, where others fear to tread . . .

Background

In undertaking the research for this book, my objective was to learn whether training really makes a difference in leadership development and, if it does, which approaches appear to be the most effective. From my undergraduate training in anthropology, I knew that the best way to investigate such a complex topic was through firsthand experience. So I selected five of the more innovative leadership training programs offered outside universities and joined them as a participant and observer. I brainstormed about vision statements with the most imaginative of participants; I leapt from ropes in trees with the most courageous of participants; and I learned the new models of leadership with the most curious of participants. In addition, my research assistants and I interviewed the managers who participated with me in the programs. From these interviews, we learned what they had found to be most effective.

Who Should Read This Book

I wrote *Learning to Lead* with a broad audience in mind. Executives, human resource professionals, trainers, consultants, and managers will find the book full of insights about the specific role that training plays in leadership development, the strategic uses of leadership training, and the effectiveness or ineffectiveness of the various training formats in use today. Those who work in academia, such as professors, deans, and directors of business schools, will find the descriptions of and suggestions for course materials especially useful. Finally, given the renewed interest in leadership in education and in public administration, professors and directors of education and public administration programs will discover valuable information for designing more innovative and more effective leadership programs.

Overview of the Contents

In Part One of *Learning to Lead,* I provide an overview of leadership training and reflect on the potential role that training can play in calling forth leadership ability. Chapter One explores the questions of how leadership training has become so popular in the last several years and why we still know so little about it. The chapter describes how current social and political events have brought leadership to the forefront as an issue of international concern and have heightened the demand for leadership skills.

Leaving aside for the moment the issue of training, in Chapter Two I consider the many roots of leadership and the proverbial question of whether leaders are born or made, because if we can understand the wellspring of leadership ability, we can develop training programs that have maximum impact.

Chapter Three discusses how organizations are currently teaching leadership. The chapter provides a historical backdrop for today's approaches by beginning with a brief history of leadership training from the time of Plato. The focus then narrows to the relatively new phenomenon of leadership training for managers and the recent transitions that are radically altering training approaches for the 1990s. I describe the new programs and organize them into a typology of four approaches: personal growth, conceptual understanding, feedback, and skill building. The five training programs examined in the book are briefly described in relation to the typology.

Part Two consists of four chapters written as diaries of experiences that either I or my research assistant Ann Latimer had in the leadership training programs we attended. They are written in a personal style so that readers get a taste of the emotions and teachings that we experienced. The diary in Chapter Four details the first of the four training approaches, personal growth. In it, I describe my experiences in two programs, the Pecos River Learning Center and ARC's VisionQuest, which seek to put participants in touch with their deeper (and presumably truer) selves. Both programs operate on the assumption that leaders are individuals who are profoundly connected to their personal dreams and talents and who act to fulfill and use them. By means of outdoor adventures and psychological exercises, these programs connect participants with their own talents, values, and desires as those relate to leading others.

The diary in Chapter Five looks at The Leadership Challenge, a program developed by James Kouzes and Barry Posner that seeks to convey to its participants an understanding of the essential qualities of leadership. Programs of this type assume that leaders-in-training can best understand the experience of leadership if they first have a conceptual overview of it. With this understanding, they can then distinguish leadership from managership and in turn find opportunities to build these different skills for themselves.

In Chapter Six, I look at how one program — the Leadership Development Program at the Center for Creative Leadership in Greensboro, North Carolina — employs an extensive feedback approach to cultivate leaders. The assumption underlying this sort of program is that many who aspire to be effective leaders already possess in varying degrees and strengths the skills they need. The aim of the program, then, is to point out to participants their own key strengths and weaknesses so that they can work to strengthen their weaker skills and can act with confidence when relying on their strengths.

When most people think of training, they think of learning skills. The skill-building approaches are the oldest in leadership training. At their core is the belief that despite its increasing complexity, leadership can still be broken down into a set of discrete behaviors that can be taught and learned. Today's programs, however, attempt to teach far more complex skills than were taught in the earlier days. So in Chapter Seven, readers will explore one of the new generation of skill-building programs, the Forum Corporation's Leadership course.

Taking a step back from the actual programs, I reflect in Part Three on the lessons learned from all these experiences. In Chapter Eight, I examine the distinct advantages and pitfalls of each of the four approaches to leadership training. Based on research interviews with fellow participants from the various programs and on my reflections on my own experiences, the chapter presents an in-depth analysis of the types of outcomes that can be expected from each approach. I spell out both the limitations and the best uses of leadership training programs. At the end of the chapter I discuss the case study of one participant who experienced a dramatic improvement in his leadership ability and examine the combination of characteristics that allowed the ultimate potential of one program to be realized.

Chapter Nine deals with the future of leadership training. By now, most managers will have joined an outdoor-adventure activity or taken the Myers-Briggs Type Indicator, so what will be next? What will leadership training be like in the future? The chapter casts a look ahead, examining curriculum designs at General Electric that may hold the key to more powerful forms of leadership training. In addition, I present the case history of Levi Strauss and Company—an organization that has been conducting some fascinating experiments with organizational systems to support and extend the impact of training—as an example of how leadership training can be used as one element in a company's overall human resource development strategy.

Finally, the appendix to the book describes the issues and complexities inherent in studying leadership training.

Acknowledgments

A research project such as this is a tremendous undertaking. *Learning to Lead* would not have been possible without the support of several organizations and individuals. Foremost among them were Dean Wallace Crowston and the Faculty of Management at McGill University, who provided the financial resources for me to conduct this project in the first place. In addition, representatives of many training organizations spent hours with me, explaining their objectives and approaches and reacting supportively to my projected critical appraisals. The individuals who critiqued my work deserve special thanks for their time and interest. Comments by Richard Boyatzis, John Kotter, Jerry LoPorto, and Mary Ann Williams on early drafts were very helpful. My research assistants were Denise Angel, Matthew Bates, Elizabeth Grant, and Ann Latimer. Each of them made an important contribution through skilled interviews or library research. Ann helped particularly, through her background research on the leadership training field and her participation in the training program described in Chapter Seven. Finally, my secretary, Pina Vicario, has been invaluable. Her industriousness and sense of organization have kept me on track and on schedule. I am especially grateful to her.

Montreal, Quebec   Jay A. Conger
May 1992

The Author

JAY A. CONGER is associate professor of organizational behavior at the Faculty of Management, McGill University, Montreal. He received his B.A. degree (1974) from Dartmouth College in anthropology, with honors, his M.B.A. degree (1977) from the University of Virginia, and his D.B.A. degree (1985) from the Harvard University Graduate School of Business Administration.

Conger consults to private and nonprofit organizations worldwide in the areas of organizational change, leadership development, and management education. His current fields of interest include executive leadership, the management of organizational change, empowerment, and the training and development of leaders and managers. He is particularly interested in how leaders foster entrepreneurship and change within their organizations and motivate their work force. Conger's books include *Charismatic Leadership* (1988, with R. N. Kanungo) and *The Charismatic Leader* (1989).

Conger is the two-time recipient (1987–88 and 1990–91) of McGill University's Distinguished Teaching Award in Management for his outstanding work as a teacher. Articles on him have appeared in *The Economist, The New York Times, Training, The Wall Street Journal, Working Woman,* and other publications.

Learning
to
Lead

Part One

Training Leaders

Chapter One

The Popular Dream:
Transforming Managers
into Leaders

*A*lways in the big woods when you leave familiar ground
and step off alone in a new place there will be, along with the
feelings of curiosity and excitement, a little nagging of dread. It
is ancient fear of the Unknown, and it is your first bond with the
wilderness you are going into. What you are doing is exploring.
— Wendell Berry

I stand nervously at the edge. I feel the solidness of the rock
supporting my feet. As my eyes glance down the cliff face, fear
tickles down my back. I am on the verge of making a decision
that moments before I had anticipated with enthusiasm. Reality is now settling in, and I feel my fear. My task is seemingly
simple: I am to leap from this ledge into a canyon that lies 125
feet below me.

My eyes follow the flow of a river that crawls past the
foot of the cliff. I am normally tranquilized by the sounds of

Epigraph from *The Unforeseen Wilderness,* copyright © 1991 by Wendell Berry.
Published by North Point Press and reprinted by permission of Farrar, Straus
& Giroux, Inc.

3

rushing water, but not today. I turn to an assistant, hoping he has some sage advice to soothe my fears. He simply smiles and says, "Look straight out, and when you are ready just put your foot off the edge." Some advice, I think to myself.

Behind my fear I sense desire for excitement and adventure. As well, I feel some hope that this experience may serve as a metaphor for issues I am facing in life — issues of risk taking in my personal life and in my career.

Then, for a moment, I remember my real purpose in being here — I am studying leadership. But what does jumping from a cliff have to do with leadership? I ask myself. With that thought in mind, I take a very deep breath. I step forward, my toes slightly over the cliff edge. I tense both legs, bend my knees, and then a second later I am over the edge.

Falling, my fear turns to excitement as a wire attached to the harness I am wearing pulls me up into the air. Stretched like a clothesline from the cliff to a post on the other side of the river, this wire transforms my fall into a glide. I glide downward toward my teammates, who stand waiting to catch me. I hear their cheers and whistles. With a sense of relief, I land and am wrapped in their arms. Again I wonder, what does all this have to do with leadership?

This is my first encounter with the new age of leadership training. I have just finished a series of outdoor activities at the Pecos River Learning Center in Pecos River, New Mexico. I have climbed a forty-foot simulated mountain face, been led blindfolded down a rocky hill, and fallen backward into the arms of fellow teammates from a height of six feet. For a grand finale, I have climbed up a telephone pole and stood on a pizza pan nailed to its top. From there, I have leapt off to catch a bell dangling from a rope some ten feet away. This is all in a day's worth of leadership training at Pecos River, one of the new wave of programs catering to North American corporations seeking ways to develop the leadership skills of their managers.

The impetus for my visit to the Pecos River Learning Center, and with the other programs I will describe in this book, was an experience I had had several years before. I had been studying executive leadership for some time and had grown increasingly aware of the complexity of many leadership skills. For example, from my research on strategic vision, I realized that vision was not something that could be taught. It was the by-product of years of experience coupled with the intuitive talents of a leader. Yet, as I conducted my research, I began to see more and more training programs offering "visioning skills." Some of these workshops even promised to teach their participants "visioning" skills within a single day! Needless to say, I was quickly becoming cynical toward leadership training. At its best, it seemed that "leadership training" was a few days of awareness building, and at its worst, a waste of money and time. After all, how could anything as complex as leadership be taught?

Then one day, a friend introduced me to a manager who had completed a leadership training program some six months before. Over lunch, I explored with her what she had learned. Surprisingly, she reported positive changes in her ability to lead others. She claimed she was no longer just managing, as she had been before; she was spending less time on administration and more time on leadership. She had set up a new vision for her organization and was active in motivating staff toward its achievement. Her subordinates' reactions confirmed her own perceptions, as compliments flowed about her new behavior. Normally, I might have attributed her comments to the seductive "high" that I knew many of the well-orchestrated training programs induced through camaraderie and adventure exercises. But she seemed the type of individual who would not easily be swayed by the hype of an enthusiastic facilitator. Feeling a bit like Alice in Wonderland, I found my view of leadership training suddenly being flipped upside down. Questioning my own skepticism, I left that lunch determined to explore the issue more seriously.

Can we, I asked myself, really hope to teach leadership? Or at least aspects of it? Or is it so complex and so based in experience or genes that trying to teach it is a futile exercise? In my new quest for answers to these questions, I sought out people who were leaders or who had studied leaders. I also started to experiment in my own classes: I shifted from presenting theories and cases to creating actual leadership experiences for my students. With clients, I used training grounded in company leadership situations.

Soon it dawned on me that the best place to learn about new approaches to leadership training would be from those who were actively using them. I wanted to experience firsthand how individuals and organizations had incorporated the newer conceptions of leadership training into innovative formats. So I set out to discover just who in North America was at the leading edge in this area. I interviewed twenty-four human resources executives, consultants, and fellow academics. A consensus quickly emerged: training organizations appeared to be doing the most interesting work. (A few individuals were also mentioned, such as Peter Block, author of *The Empowered Manager,* and Stephen R. Covey, author of *The Seven Habits of Highly Effective People.*) I was surprised that corporate or graduate business programs were not more frequently mentioned, but the opinion prevailed that their conservative natures precluded much innovation. There were, however, references to innovative work in the academic sphere at places like the State University of New York at Binghamton, the University of Chicago, the University of Michigan, the Wharton School at the University of Pennsylvania, and the University of Virginia, but these were described as a distinct minority. As well, many of my sources felt that universities did not operate under the Darwinian marketplace pressures that force training organizations to offer tangible and immediate training results. Whether these impressions were fully accurate or not, I ultimately decided to focus my energies on the vendor programs rather than on individuals or on university and in-house corporate programs.

Out of my interviews, I eventually identified five leadership programs as consistently innovative and specifically focused on leadership development. All were programs that managers and executives in charge of corporate training perceived as being at the leading edge, and all would be among their first choices for implementation in their own corporations. Fortunately, also, the five programs proved to be diverse in their approaches. They ranged from simple skill building to intensive feedback to conceptual overviews to personal growth approaches. Thus, in surveying these five, I could look at a wide variety of training formats. It is important to note that the selection of this "sample" in no way reflects on the caliber of other leadership training programs. There are undoubtedly other programs that are as innovative as those described here, or even more so. They were, however, either not offered at the time of the study or were not brought to my attention. Therefore, readers should not assume that these five are "the best" — rather, that they are among the better known.

Finally, I decided that the only way to learn about the effectiveness of these programs was to join them as an active participant, in true anthropological fashion. I could then judge firsthand what seemed to work and what did not. As a result, in the better moments of these programs, I felt myself stretched as well as deeply challenged. With my fellow participants, I would jump off cliffs, formulate personal vision statements, reflect on my life, and do many hair-raising and unusual things. In the lesser moments of these programs, I was reminded of how painful it can be to sit through hours of lecture. Needless to say, I returned to the classroom with new empathy for my students and clients. That alone was worth the investment of time and energy in the project.

In critiquing these programs, I relied not only on my own perceptions of a program but also on those of my fellow participants, who became my research barometers for a program's effectiveness. After exercises, I would survey them for personal reactions. When my sojourns had all ended, my research assistant and I interviewed this group of approximately one hundred fifty managers who had participated with me, to learn their perspectives on leadership training and personal development (see the Appendix). This book is my record of what I learned and what I observed others learning from these experiences. It constitutes my exploration of the question, can we hope to teach leadership abilities? It is a highly personal book. It reflects the odyssey of an individual who has long loved the art of teaching and the excitement of new adventures. For me, this project has been a wonderful journey.

When I started out, I remembered a story that I had read

about the magician Harry Houdini. After his mother's death, he became intrigued by the idea of an afterlife. He visited numerous clairvoyants who claimed they could contact his dead mother. He was suspicious, however. So he set out with his own scientific methods to discover who were the frauds and who were the true clairvoyants. It became a passion for him, this mysterious world of the occult.

For me, the story of Houdini's quest is analogous to my search for effective leadership training. There are many individuals and organizations who claim that they have the special ability to transform managers into leaders. Some have elegant models and fancy settings, much like the parlors of Houdini's spiritual advisors. Others are more realistic about the art of leadership training and rely on pragmatic long-term approaches. Like Houdini, I set out to visit and investigate those who seemed to be actually training leaders and those whose "smoke and mirrors" simply created an illusion of that. As the reader, you will be joining with me in that exploration.

The Times They Are A-Changing

This is the most exciting time to explore the issue of leadership development since the decade following World War II. Two important trends occurring over the 1970s and 1980s have produced a radical shift in the way we perceive leadership, and as a result, they have challenged traditional methods of teaching leadership. The first is a newfound *interest* in the idea of leadership itself. The second is an accompanying radical shift in what we know about the *process* of leadership.

Competitive challenges in the 1980s forced many North American companies to reexamine the ways they had organized themselves. Years of success had yielded growth, but also deeply layered bureaucracy. Stiflingly slow and conservative decision making by the hierarchy was killing responsiveness to markets. In addition, more and more chief executives were being drawn from the ranks of finance. As a consequence, companies were now managed more like financial portfolios rather than product portfolios. In the face of invasions by Japanese and European companies, American corporations suddenly looked far less competitive. This disastrous hardening of corporate arteries prompted the press, business schools, and corporations to reexamine management effectiveness. Attention turned to leadership as one of the key factors.

As the lack of leadership became apparent in our traditional industries, its vital presence in other sectors grabbed media attention. For while some industries were dying, others were growing dramatically. The business environment of the 1960s and 1970s saw a flowering of new products and services, from silicon semiconductor chips to McDonald's hamburgers. Most of these new products had an entrepreneur behind them. The vision, flair, and drive of these individuals drew national attention as the public began to search for reassurance that North America had not lost its touch. Computer whiz kids like Steve Jobs of Apple Computer and Bill Gates of Microsoft became national heros. Lee Iaccoca's turnaround of the Chrysler Corporation led to a campaign to draft him for the United States presidency. Business leaders were becoming pop stars in their own right, and for the first time in decades, books about business leaders were now best-sellers.

On the political front, also, leadership was foremost in our minds. The 1960s had ushered in two charismatic leaders, John F. Kennedy in the United States and Pierre Trudeau in Canada. For a while in these two countries, people seemed to sense a glorious destiny. Soon, however, Richard Nixon, with his scandal-riddled Watergate affair, and Jimmy Carter, with his stalled presidency, sent the idea of leadership into disrepute. The 1980s brought a spurt of renewed excitement, as Mikhail Gorbachev, Ronald Reagan, and Margaret Thatcher took charge in their respective nations. But by the early 1990s, leadership seemed again on a downward track, as Gorbachev lost control of Russia, Reagan's economic policies proved exorbitant, and Thatcher retired amid national criticism.

These last three decades, then, have seen a remarkable display of the best and worst of leadership at all levels, in organizations and in society. At the same time, management practitioners and academics were revising their views of just what leadership was. Indeed, the new theories and approaches introduced during the 1980s represented a revolution in our conception of leadership.

Terms like *charisma, transformational, vision, mission, inspiration,* and *empowerment* appeared. They were a sharp contrast to the leadership language of the 1960s, which included words like *participative, people oriented, supportive,* and *task oriented.* The new words seemed to convey an underlying restlessness with ordinary management and a deeply felt need for revitalization across society's institutions.

Earlier, the term *leader* had been applied loosely to anyone who was managing others, and academics had divided leadership roles into two simple ones: a social role and a task role.[1] The social role constituted a leader's ability to show a "people-oriented" concern for subordinates by building mutual trust, developing good interpersonal relations, being sensitive to feelings, and being open to suggestions. The task role, on the other hand, described a leader's ability to define and structure the various tasks and roles of subordinates in order to achieve organizational goals.[2] This two-dimensional approach to leadership became the underlying model for most of the leadership training programs of the 1960s and 1970s, as exemplified by the popularity of programs such as the Managerial Grid.[3]

By the 1980s, however, dissatisfaction with these earlier models was growing. They seemed too narrow and sterile. How could something as rich as leadership be captured in two dimensions? As well, a new generation of leadership researchers turned their attention to the executive levels, whereas earlier studies had focused on the shop floor. As researchers explored the executive suite, they found leadership to be more complex. Their studies shifted attention to such new areas as vision, inspirational communications, and the management of radical change. A major transition was under way. Leadership training would soon feel its impact, for the new perspectives would profoundly alter existing approaches.

As training organizations began to incorporate the newer models of leadership, their programs moved away from the simple task and social dimensions to an array of new skills. Indeed, the process of training changed fundamentally. Managers were no longer sitting in classrooms, listening to management theory; they instead were scaling mountains, jumping off cliffs, working on actual company projects, and formulating vision statements for themselves and their companies. They also explored their personal lives on the assumption that leadership came "from within." The context and content of leadership training changed radically.

These changes were not due merely to new academic insights into what constituted leadership; there were other important influences. The first was the incorporation of training experiences from outdoor-adventure programs, such as Outward Bound. Originally designed as "rites of passage" for young adults, these wilderness programs exposed participants to challenges in the out-of-doors. Small groups of teammates faced various outdoor adventures, such as climbing mountains, canoeing whitewater rapids, or hiking great distances. These tasks challenged each individual's courage, strength of character, and interpersonal skills. Lessons about the necessity of teamwork and leadership were a natural by-product.

As the baby boomers moved beyond their teenage years, organizations like Outward Bound grew concerned about a shrinking market for their courses. Shorter programs were introduced for older adults, some of whom were managers and executives. By the 1970s, Outward Bound found itself offering customized programs to help build teamwork in organizations. Copycat organizations quickly sprang up offering outdoor-adventure programs solely for the corporate markets. And by the end of the 1980s, many managers could say that they had rappelled down cliffs or walked on tightwires strung high among the trees, all in the name of leadership training and teamwork building.

At the same time that outdoor programs were making their impact on management education, the New Age movement was having its influence. Individuals involved in the "human potential" movement were like traders, bringing their goods — their training technologies — to new management markets. Programs such as Erhard Seminar Training (est) and Lifespring (both of which required participants to face psychological challenges in order to explore their inner selves) would soon spin off leadership training programs. Out of est came the Forum, and out of Lifespring came ARC International, founded by Robert White, president and cofounder of Lifespring. Like Outward Bound, these programs were initially designed for private individuals, but by the late 1970s, their original markets were saturated. With limited growth in sight and a business community searching for new ideas, the next and natural market for the human potential movement was the corporate world.

While innovations involving the human potential movement and outdoor programs were evolving, human resource professionals in corporations began to seriously struggle with the problem of transferring learning from the classroom to the job. Managers might learn and exhibit leadership abilities in a simulation, but back on the job such abilities often evaporated. In response to this dilemma, "action learning" became the new orientation. "Action" meant focusing on real problems in the company by employing the new skills participants were learning. For example, in a course that focused on the development of strategy skills, participating managers would investigate and find solutions to strategic issues the company was actually facing. Training was becoming more relevant.

The forces that emerged in the 1980s dramatically altered leadership training in the 1990s and left the managerial grids of the 1960s looking quite simplistic. But, as in any time of change, it is difficult to see what will be of lasting value and what will be passing fads. Like Houdini's dilemma, it is not clear which approaches are truly effective. Certainly training has seen its share of fads, from creative problem solving to assertiveness training, and these times are no different.

But before we begin to understand the value of the new training approaches to leadership development, we must first visit the issue of the origins of leadership itself. For if, as some argue, leadership is a product of an individual's heredity, then training programs can offer us little. They are at best just another in a series of "snake oil" remedies for effective leadership development. If, however, leadership ability is the outcome of life's experiences *and* the learning of skills, then training may actually play a role in a leader's development. The woman manager with whom I had lunch may just have been right. Depending on which approach is more accurate, training may have no role whatsoever or a vital role. Our first step is to answer the question, where do leaders come from?

Chapter Two

Born or Made?
Forces That Foster
Leadership

I doubted at first whether I should attempt the creation of a being like myself, or one of much simpler organization; but my imagination was too much exalted . . . to permit me to doubt of my ability to give life to an animal as complex and wonderful as a man. . . .

It was on a dreary night of November that I beheld the accomplishment of my toils. With an anxiety that almost amounted to agony, I collected the instruments of life around me, that I might infuse a spark of being into the lifeless thing that lay at my feet. It was already one in the morning; the rain pattered dismally against the panes, and my candle was nearly burnt out, when, by the glimmer of the half-extinguished light, I saw the dull yellow eye of the creature; it breathed hard, and a convulsive motion agitated its limbs.

— Mary Shelley

When I think about the idea of leadership training and the origins of leadership, I am reminded of Mary Shelley's character, Dr. Frankenstein. Here was an individual trying to meld together bits and pieces of human bodies and spark them into life. Through their various experiences, leadership training programs are attempting to graft onto managers the abilities of effective

14

leaders—a task somewhat analogous to though less hair-raising than the quest of Shelley's doctor. Given the array of training programs and the considerable funds expended for them, it is clear that many believe we can simply "create" leaders. And, of course, there is no shortage of approaches—and practically all make the same assumption: that leaders are made.

Scholars of leadership are more divided as to whether leaders are born or made. Some of us argue that genetics and childhood dynamics are the forces behind leaders. Others see life experiences as the critical factors. These perspectives are quite different, and their implications for the training and development of leaders are profoundly different. If leadership ability is genetically determined, training could hardly play a role in its development. But if leadership is learned through experience, training might well be used to develop new skills and to help synthesize past experiences into useful insights.

In joining this debate, we encounter a crucial lack of rigorous, longitudinal studies of leaders that might prove one or the other point of view. Without such studies, we have no accurate measure of the forces that have shaped these individuals. The topic remains full of speculation, enlightened by very little hard evidence. Unfortunately, what Warren Bennis wrote in 1959 about our understanding of leadership remains true today: "Of all the hazy and confounding areas in social psychology, leadership theory undoubtedly contends for top nomination. And, ironically, probably more has been written and less known about leadership than any other topic in the behavioral sciences. Always, it seems the concept of leadership eludes us or turns up in another form to taunt us again with its slipperiness and complexity."[1]

This is not to say that little progress has been made since 1959. If we make an analogy to scientists trying to puzzle out the universe, we might say that our knowledge of certain "galaxies" of leadership behavior has improved dramatically. For instance, we understand that the ability to formulate a strategic vision is a critical skill for many forms of leadership. Yet, we are still uncertain about the ultimate "universe" of factors that determine a leader's capabilities. For example, what role does context play in fostering a person's status as a leader? In this chapter, we explore an aspect of the leadership "universe" that is perhaps the least understood: the origins of leadership. With this done, we can begin to put the issues of training for leadership skills in perspective.

Who Becomes a Leader?

I am standing in a hotel lobby in North Carolina waiting for a van to take myself and some twenty other people to the Center for Creative Leadership. We have just arrived for the Center's five-day leadership training program. I am talking to a woman manager who has asked me, "Where do leaders come from?" I answer as best I can, mentioning something about certain behaviors and experiences. The van arrives and we climb in. Turning her question over in my mind, I look at my fellow participants. I begin to wonder whether I can detect the individuals who are more likely than others to become leaders during the course of this week.

I notice Ed, at the wheel. With great gusto and assertiveness, he has volunteered to drive. Lightheartedly, I wonder if this demonstration reflects deeper leadership abilities. There is Deborah, to my right—a dynamic woman full of energy and good humor. She has quickly engaged me in conversation, and I find myself impressed by her commanding personality. Again, I wonder, leader? Bruno, in the back, is quiet and seems shy. I think to myself, limited leadership potential there.

Next to Ed are Jackie, from Jamaica, and Christian, from Washington, D.C. They are engaged in animated conversation about Jamaica. Jackie is a petite brunette, with eyes of great intensity. I recall the comments of a political scientist who once told me that intense eyes were a distinguishing characteristic of charismatic leaders. I ponder whether we have a charismatic leader in our midst. Christian, on the other hand, is a tall, physically imposing man with a deep, rich voice. He definitely has the physical potential, I think, remembering the early leadership studies that had shown height and looks to be important. His ringing voice is reminiscent of Martin Luther King, Jr.'s.

The language skills are probaby there, I suspect. There are several others in the van, but they seem shy and inclined to admire the view. I lightheartedly say to myself that clearly these other individuals would have a difficult time becoming leaders.

This vanful of individuals is a sort of microcosm, I realize, of the infinite variety of personalities among managers. How many, though, have the potential to lead? From first impressions, it seems clear that several possess certain qualities conducive to leading. I think back to the stereotypes I have of leaders and potential leaders. Energy, height, a commanding voice, intelligence, signs of assertiveness — these are all the outward signs of leadership, supposedly. But are these qualities enough?

As the week progresses, I am surprised to see who emerge as leaders from our vanful of individuals. It soon becomes clear that possessing the stereotypic traits is no guarantee of leadership. Christian, for example, defers leadership responsibilities to others; in most of our exercises, he lets others take charge. Jackie is so facilitative that her own opinions never emerge. Ed has antagonized many of us with his attempts to dominate our group — efforts that are met with firm resistance. Bruno proves to be the surprise. His quietness was not shyness; he acts decisively and has gained the respect of our entire group. Deborah has also become a leader in the group. Her presence and style of directing we find effective and worthy of our followership.

From this little experiment, I reflect on the question first asked me: Where do leaders come from? It is clear that simply possessing certain traits associated with leadership is no guarantee that one will emerge a leader. Second, one must be motivated to lead. Christian, for example, possessed many "leader" traits, yet he consistently deferred to others. He lacked the motivation to lead. Third, the leadership role can be conferred by followers, but they cannot be forced to grant it. Ed, for example, tried to take the lead by dominating the group, but he was never awarded leadership status. Leaders must understand the needs and values of their potential followers — a complex skill among the many complexities of the leadership process. I ask myself, how and where did Bruno and Deborah develop their capacity for this difficult and delicate business?

Defining Leadership

Let me begin by arguing that leadership is largely an intuitive concept for which there can never be a single, agreed-upon definition. Burt Nanus and Warren Bennis in their book *Leaders* reported some three hundred and fifty definitions of leadership that leadership researchers had generated over the last thirty years.[2] After the most extensive review ever made of the leadership literature, Ralph Stogdill concluded, "There are almost as many definitions of leadership as there are persons who have attempted to define the concept."[3]

Leadership has been defined in terms of individual traits, behaviors, influence over others, interaction patterns, role relationships, hierarchical position, and the perception of others regarding the legitimacy of influence.[4] As well, quite a number of conceptions have been based on studies of people we would today call managers rather than leaders. Thus our definitions are not always formulated to describe the same behaviors or concepts. It is no surprise, then, that there is little agreement about the term. Rather than be caught in a debate of viewpoints, I have chosen to use a single definition that is broad enough to capture many of the important manifestations of leadership in organizations and that also outlines the general behaviors that we would seek to develop:

> Leaders are individuals who establish direction for
> a working group of individuals, who gain commit-
> ment from these group members to this direction,
> and who then motivate these members to achieve
> the direction's outcomes.

For many reasons, such a broad definition as this one is preferable because it allows the multiple permutations of leadership to emerge. As a friend of mine likes to say, there are several ways up Mount Everest. So it is with leaders: one can simply compare Robert Allen of American Telephone & Telegraph and Jack Welch of General Electric — two very different individuals and yet two successful leaders.

To borrow from John Kotter's work *A Force for Change,* three dimensions of the leadership of complex organizations naturally flow from this definition: (1) establishing direction, (2) aligning people in terms of that direction, and (3) motivating and inspiring people to move in that direction.[5] (Exhibit 2.1 describes in detail these functions and their outcomes, in contrast to managerial behavior.) These functions can take many forms. Setting direction can range from devising a company's strategic mission to establishing production goals for a manufacturing unit. In other words, they cover the span from grand to mundane.[6]

A person need not perform all three functions to be perceived as a leader. For example, in some contexts a leader may principally provide direction. An extreme example of this would be "idea leadership," in which individuals lead others to see or understand the world in new ways (for example, philosophers, scientists, artists). Followers of such a leader are not so much an organized group as a general public or, perhaps, a loosely affiliated society or professional group. At the other end of the spectrum is a factory supervisor who has little or no responsibility for defining his or her group's overall goals, but who nonetheless actively leads by gaining commitment and motivating subordinates to achieve these goals. Leadership, then, is not restricted to the management of an organization or to a particular level in a hierarchy.

Are Leaders Born or Made?

There is some agreement among researchers that genetics and childhood must play a role in the development of leadership abilities.[7] Where the debate flares up is in the degree to which they play the determining role. The "born-leader school" argues that genes and childhood are the overwhelming forces behind leadership. Implicit in this point of view is an assumption that the "right" genes and the "right" family are relatively rare, and that this rarity explains why we see so few leaders.

Exhibit 2.1. Comparing Management and Leadership.

Activity	Management	Leadership
Creating an agenda	Planning and Budgeting — establishing detailed steps and timetables for achieving needed results, and then allocating the resources necessary to achieve those results.	Establishing Direction — developing a vision of the future, often the distant future, along with strategies for producing the changes needed to achieve that vision
Developing a human network for achieving the agenda	Organizing and Staffing — establishing some structure for accomplishing plan requirements, staffing that structure with individuals, delegating responsibility and authority for carrying out the plan, providing policies and procedures to help guide people, and creating methods or systems to monitor implementation	Aligning People — communicating the direction by words and deeds to all those whose cooperation may be needed so as to influence the creation of teams and coalitions that understand the vision and strategies and accept their validity
Execution	Controlling and Problem Solving — monitoring results vs. plan in some detail, identifying deviations, and then planning and organizing to solve these problems	Motivating and Inspiring — energizing people to overcome major political, bureaucratic, and resource barriers to change by satisfying very basic, but often unfulfilled, human needs
Outcomes	Produces a degree of predictability and order, and has the potential of consistently producing key results expected by various stakeholders (e.g., for customers, always being on time; for stockholders, being on budget)	Produces change, often to a dramatic degree, and has the potential of producing extremely useful change (e.g., new products that customers want, new approaches to labor relations that help make a firm more competitive)

Source: Adapted from John P. Kotter, *A Force for Change: How Leadership Differs from Management* (New York: Free Press, 1990). Reprinted with permission.

Genetic Predisposition for Leadership

Surprisingly, there is some support for the idea that genetics may play an important role. Certainly, two qualities often described in leadership studies — intelligence and physical energy — appear to have genetic roots. More interestingly, studies conducted on identical twins reared in different families hint that certain personality traits associated with leadership could be inherited. A long-term study at the University of Minnesota that focused on eleven personality traits discovered that more than half the variation in traits was due to heredity in the majority of the cases. Intriguing from the perspective of leadership is the fact that a particular trait called *social potency* — an individual's ability to be masterful and to be a forceful leader — had 61 percent of its variation explained by heredity. A second trait, *harm avoidance,* may be associated with leadership, and also had significant ties to genetics. Inversely related to the leader's ability to take risks, this trait marks an individual's desire to shun the excitement of risk and danger, to prefer the safe route, even if it is tedious; 51 percent of its variance was explained by heredity.[8] Unfortunately, this is the only such study. It has not been duplicated by others as yet. Thus, it would be premature to say with authority that genetics is a key determinant of leadership. Harvard psychologist Howard Gardner's comments on the results of the twin study also capture the dilemma of drawing too firm a conclusion: "Scientists eyeing the same set of data — and not even disputing the data — can reach widely divergent conclusions about heritability. . . . [for example] some scientists would place the heritability of intelligence as high as 80 percent. . . . Other scientists pondering the same data but operating on different assumptions would estimate heritability at less than 20 percent or even zero. . . . There is considerable agreement that physical traits are most straightforwardly genetic, that aspects of temperament are also largely genetic; but when it comes to aspects of cognitive style or personality, the case for high heritability is far less convincing."[9]

Assume, however, for a moment that genes actually predispose an individual to become a leader. If we return to the three functions of leaders (setting direction, aligning followers, and motivating followers), how might genetics play a role? All three capacities might well rest on certain forms of intelligence that may have biological roots. For example, direction setting may depend on a cognitive ability to think out problems over long time spans and to process and simplify complex information.[10] The other two behaviors — aligning and motivating — may be tied to what Harvard psychologist Howard Gardner calls "personal intelligences," or the ability to read the intentions and motivations of individuals.[11] Genetics could then predetermine one's capacity for these forms of intelligence.

Even so, experience would still play a critical role. For example, a child is not capable of devising effective strategies for a food products company. While the unformed ability may be in place, it cannot be effectively utilized without a base of knowledge. An analogy would be an individual born with the proper musculature to become a successful athlete. Without effective coaching and training, this individual's athletic potential would remain forever underdeveloped. Experience provides a foundation of knowledge that can be used by an individual who has the native ability to think strategically. For example, Harvard psychologist Daniel Isenberg discovered that what managers called their "intuition" in making effective business decisions was in reality a decision-making capacity based on years of trial-and-error experiences in similar situations. From these experiences, they had learned what actions were effective. The cumulative information formed what they were calling "intuition." Experience, however, provided that critical base of knowledge.[12]

Childhood Experiences and the Family

If we move beyond genes to the forces of early childhood in the leadership equation, we find other factors that might come into play. For example, John Gardner consulted with distinguished child psychologists on the born-leader issue. This is how Gardner described their "speculative" responses: "Physical vitality and intelligence [of a leader] are probably primarily genetic, but intelligence is very likely influenced quite substantially by early childhood experience with respect to language usage. . . . The capacity to understand others and skill in dealing with others has its most striking development in adolescence and especially young adulthood, but the beginnings are in the years before five. The need for achievement is probably formed by experiences in the first year of life. . . . Confidence and assertiveness are formed early, but they are situation specific. The child may be confident or assertive in certain contexts and not in others."[13]

So while child psychologists would agree that genes play a role, it is childhood conditioning that lays the more important groundwork for leadership. Families are in essence cultivating the child's intellect, interests, and talents, and they are the first role models for interpersonal skills. As such, their actions may directly affect the future leader's ability to think strategically, to be articulate, and to motivate and align others.

The family also sets expectations for the child's later achievements and success. Through their demonstrations of love and praise, parents powerfully influence the child's sense of self-esteem. Taken together, these actions may address a critical element of the leadership equation: from where springs the desire to become a leader? Families may prove to be the source for the motivation to lead. And we may find that a home of never-ending high expectations and inadequate love may be just as conducive as one with a strong base of love and well-measured expectations. (For example, always striving to be a success in order to meet the never-ending expectations of a demanding parent — and to finally win that parent's esteem — may provide enormous motivational energy for some future leaders.)

Reflecting on the motivation to lead, political scientist James McGregor Burns comments, "Two powerful influences play on adolescents, drawing some of them into positions of potential leadership and keeping others out. . . . One is a continuing need for self-esteem. . . . The second is a developing need and capacity for social role-taking."[14] Burns goes so far to say that "one generalization seems safe on the basis of systematic and casual observation: the most potent sources of political motivation . . . are unfulfilled esteem needs (both self-esteem and esteem by others). These do not have to be pathological; some individuals simply have strong needs. And according to James David Barber, who studied political leaders, two types of individuals were likely to be drawn into leadership contests: 'those who have such high self-esteem that they can manage relatively easily the threats and strains and anxieties involved . . . and those who have such low self-esteem that they are ready to do this extraordinary thing to raise it.'"[15]

Normally this striving for self-esteem should create a needy individual with little appeal. Yet in most of us, it is balanced by a capacity to empathize with others because the search for power, beginning in childhood, occurs within a social system — the family — that encourages us to identify our strivings for self-esteem within the strivings of a larger social group. "Thus the striving for self-esteem and the evolution of a sense of human empathy," Burns notes, "work in harmony to bring out the potential for leadership."[16]

Family dynamics may, therefore, give life to the quest for leadership by shaping these esteem needs early on in life. But again, like the potential athlete, these require a context and a baseline of skills to manifest themselves into actual leading. They may be the motivating spark to lead, but as we saw with my fellow participant Ed at the Center for Creative Leadership, his wish to lead was not the same as our wanting him to lead.

There may be other needs related to the desire to lead that are tied to childhood, such as needs for self-actualization or individuality. The self-actualization need may be especially important in enabling leaders to understand their followers. "I suggest . . . it is their capacity to learn from others and the environment. . . . It is this kind of self-actualization that enables leaders to comprehend the needs of potential followers, to enter into their perspectives, and to act on popular needs," proposes Burns.[17] Family dynamics may contribute to the development of self-actualization needs when parents encourage active learning, curiosity, and personal growth. Alternatively, childhood traumas may also spark these needs as individuals strive to overcome emotional pain through personal growth experiences.

Individuality needs, on the other hand, may explain why

certain people are willing to assume the risks associated with leadership, such as breaking from conventions or taking bold, visionary stands. Some psychiatrists have argued that the unconventionality associated with certain leaders arises specifically from the need to create a special identity. An important contributor to this school of thought is American psychologist William James, who formulated a theory of basic personality types called the "once-borns" and the "twice-borns."[18]

The once-borns, James argued, were individuals who experienced the flow of life as reasonably straightforward from the moment of birth. Their family life was harmonious and peaceful. Twice-borns, however, were faced with great struggles. Their lives were never easy, and unlike once-borns, they could take little for granted. As a result, the two personalities developed very different worldviews.

Once-borns felt few compulsions to be different from others or to act in ways that were a departure from the norm. Twice-borns, in contrast, felt a profound sense of separateness. Because of this, they experienced little dependency on their organizations, their work roles, or on others. They tended to feel little or no desire to adhere to the status quo or to follow other's directives. Instead, the twice-borns felt free to promote change and to lead people in new directions. Along with certain aptitudes and personal expectations of achievement, their self-reliance set them in motion to become leaders. Then, with the selective influence of mentors and others late in life, they would gain a foothold in positions of leadership.[19]

The principal proponent of this argument, Abraham Zaleznik, argues that the differences are especially clear when contrasting leaders with managers:

> Leaders grow through mastering painful conflict during their developmental years, while managers confront few of the experiences that generally cause people to turn inward. Managers perceive life as a steady progression of positive events, resulting in security at home, in school, in the community, and at work. Leaders are "twice-born" individuals

who endure major events that lead to a sense of
separateness, or perhaps, estrangement from their
environment. As a result they turn inward in order
to reemerge with a created rather than an inherited
sense of identity. That sense of separateness may
be a necessary condition for the ability to lead.[20]

While such arguments are appealing, there are aspects
of the theory that appear incomplete. For example, proponents
of this school provide few details about the exact character of
the twice-borns' family situations. We know that the twice-born
child develops a feeling of being special and a sense of having
to struggle — but what types of parent-child relations are necessary to create this condition? I suspect that the permutations
are so numerous that it is impossible to specify them all.

And what is meant by "struggle"? Some specify the struggle as "inner conflict," but, again, the type of inner conflict is
often left vague.[21] As well, inner psychological conflict is a universal phenomenon, so how do we identify the specific inner
conflicts that facilitate the development of leadership? In addition, what if we were to discover that the twice-born family environment is actually quite commonplace? How could we then
explain why so few twice-born people go on to become leaders?
There would have to be other factors.

Moreover, it seems a fine line between a childhood of
struggle that breeds self-confidence and one that destroys self-
confidence. If we take the logic to an extreme, we might argue
that children from hardship environments would be prime candidates for leadership. Yet most of our leaders come from the
better-educated, financially secure classes. Perhaps the most instructive challenges to any theory's viability are found in exceptions. Based on biographical information, one of the most
visible exceptions to the theory appears to be Franklin D. Roosevelt. His biographer, renowned leadership researcher James
MacGregor Burns, concluded:

He was no product of a broken home or of a ruined
land. He knew nothing of family strife, physical

want, contemptuous glances. His father "never laughed at him. . . ." He adored his parents, and as an only child he never suffered even the common experience of dethronement by younger children. . . . His environment laid no stress on competitive achievement in business or politics. He was to be a Hyde Park gentleman.

   Was the pursuit of power in Franklin's genes? . . . On the Roosevelt side there is the striking fact that, after six generations of unremarkable men, "in the seventh generation, this dynasty of the mediocre suddenly blazed up with not one but two of the most remarkable men in history [Theodore and Franklin Roosevelt]. . . . Most of the Delanos [maternal side] passed politics by; they were shipowners, merchants. . . .

   Did James and Sara Roosevelt, by design or by chance, fashion a world for their son that would encourage an interest in politics? One looks in vain for any such evidence. It was not a world of envy, ambition, or power. . . . It was a world with deep roots in the American past, asking nothing for the future except a gracious life and a secure estate on the banks of the Hudson.[22]

Personally, I am not convinced of the twice-born theory. Its popularity lies in its elegant simplicity, which is seductive. Remember, however, that James was a social scientist whose aim was to construct theory. His theory of personality was not meant as an accurate picture of reality, but as a conceptual tool. In the real world, most people are somewhere along a continuum between the once-born and twice-born types. It is not possible for such a model to capture the complexity of human life. And even proponents of the born-leader school argue that childhood experiences do not explain enough; later developmental experiences such as mentors may be equally important.[23]

   I would add a final word on the born-leader argument. One of the important leadership questions that this school is attempting to answer is, What is it about a leader's personality that allows him or her to break from the status quo? The theory assumes that leaders are norm-breakers, and the question it directly addresses concerns the first of the leadership qualities we discussed earlier—setting direction. It is assumed that managers, on the one hand, adhere to the status quo and are therefore unable to set new directions. Leaders, on the other hand, are risk takers because they deeply believe in themselves and are unafraid of others' expectations. Their "twice-born" sense of separateness gives them the freedom to take an unconventional stand.

If we isolate out this particular disposition and ask ourselves, Does this factor have its roots in childhood? we find it intuitively appealing to say yes. However, could we not expect to see such individuals exhibiting this behavior throughout their lives if this were the case? Individuals like Churchill certainly prove the argument, yet are there exceptions? I am aware of at least one leader who was anything but a risk taker until quite late in his life. Although his biography is poorly documented, we know that Archbishop Cesar Romero of El Salvador spent most of his career as politically cautious priest. It was not until the assassination of his priest friends by government death squads that he began to take radical stands and became a populist leader. In his case, external circumstances, rather than a seemingly profound sense of "separateness" from childhood, encouraged him to take risks. Apparently, the events of later life may well serve as catalysts for leadership.

The following conclusions might be drawn about the born-leader school. In a majority of cases, family environments may serve as catalysts for the need or motivation to lead. They may also encourage the development of certain intellectual and interpersonal skills required by leaders. And of the many permutations of family environments, some may be more conducive to the development of leadership drive and ability than others. I use the plural term *some environments* because I believe numerous contexts are probably conducive; simply compare Hitler's and Roosevelt's families. They are diametrically opposed, yet both produced leaders. Hitler's father, a civil servant, was a petty tyrant who bullied and beat his wife and child. Roosevelt's father was a benevolent man who was a risk-taking business tycoon. While Hitler met head-on with the difficulties of life, Roosevelt stayed insulated within a world of wealth. It seems that we are not likely to find a single "best" family dynamic. Just as there is no one leadership personality, so there can be no one family structure that produces leaders.

As with the issue of genes, we must ask ourselves, are these family environments rare? Probably not — that is, relative to the rarity of good leaders. Yet implicit in the born-leader school is the assumption that the "right" genes or the "right" family dynamics are rare, and this rarity explains why we see so few leaders. What if, instead, we were to find that there exists a significant proportion of the population with the "right" genes and family environment? Why is it, then, that a proportionately large pool of potential leaders dwindles down to only a few? This question, I believe, is best answered by the "leadership-is-learned" school.

Adult Experiences That Catalyze Leadership

The majority of leadership researchers believe that the origins of leadership go beyond genes and family to other sources. Work experiences, hardship, opportunity, education, role models, and mentors all go together to craft a leader. Within their argument also lies the assumption that the potential to lead is not uncommon; the scarcity of actual leaders is a reflection of neglected development rather than of a dearth of abilities.

Two recent works are particularly important in shedding light on the leadership-is-learned argument. Morgan McCall, Michael Lombardo, and Ann Morrison studied 191 successful executives to determine what forces were behind their success. (Note the implicit assumption that successful executives are of necessity leaders, an assumption that some might question.) As their conclusion clearly states, experience was the common denominator in the ability of all of these individuals to lead: "People who emerge as candidates for executive jobs may come with a lot of givens, but what happens to them on the job matters.

Knowledge of how the business works, ability to work with senior executives, learning to manage governments, handling tense political situations, firing people — these and many others are the lessons of experience. They are taught on the firing line, by demanding assignments, by good and bad bosses, and by mistakes and setbacks and misfortune. Maybe executives are blessed with characteristics that give them the edge in learning these things, but learn them they must."[24]

In addition, John Kotter surveyed two hundred executives at highly successful companies and interviewed in depth twelve individuals who demonstrated highly effective leadership. He concluded that early in their careers his leaders had opportunities to lead, to take risks, and to learn from their successes and failures. He specifically identified the following as important developmental opportunities: (1) challenging assignments early in a career, (2) visible leadership role models who were either very good or very bad, (3) assignments that broadened knowledge and experience, (4) task force assignments, (5) mentoring or coaching from senior executives, (6) attendance at meetings outside a person's core responsibility, (7) special development jobs (executive assistant jobs), (8) special projects, and (9) formal training programs.[25] The breadth of perspective gained through these opportunities eventually contributed to effective leadership, including, specifically, setting a direction for the organization and aligning and motivating subordinates. Through their early successes and failures, these executives learned important lessons about how future actions should be taken.

From these two studies, certain types of work experiences emerge as the primary developmental forces behind leadership. For example, challenging and multifunctional work assignments taught self-confidence, toughness, persistence, knowledge of the business, skill in managing relationships, a sense of independence, and leadership. Hardship taught personal limits and strengths, while success bred confidence and an understanding of one's distinct skills. Diversity in experiences developed breadth and perspective on the business and in human relations. Bosses modeled managerial and human values and taught the lessons of politics. This total mix set the stage for leadership ability.[26] In addition, luck often played a role. A job opening or an unexpected emergency situation may have provided chances to learn as well as to demonstrate leadership—and the visibility that ensured future opportunities to lead. Napoleon, for example, started out as a novelist—a mediocre one at that. It was only after entering the military later in his life that his talents as a military strategist emerged. His luck was to be drafted.

Personal Desire and the Willingness to Lead

The leadership-is-learned school operates on the assumption that many possess the potential to lead. The many dwindle down to a few only because most of us do not have the right opportunities or experiences. For instance, organizational factors play a critical role. Companies that do not provide for challenging job assignments early in one's career or that fail to offer assignments that broaden or expose one to leadership role models may not be conducive to leadership development. Clearly, there are rare exceptions; for example, a company may suddenly find itself in a highly competitive situation, and a new president is appointed. This individual is not in the least worried about leadership training, yet the crisis provides a wonderful opportunity for hands-on leadership development for employees.

The issue is more complex, however. It is clear from my own experience that some managers choose not to use their leadership ability, even those with a backlog of experiences. Richard Boyatzis noticed a similar phenomenon:

> Over twenty years of experience conducting competency studies in organizations, especially on middle management and executive jobs, focused my attention on the top 3 percent of the job holders in any organization who appeared to be truly outstanding in all aspects of the job. Frequently, I made the observation that many more individuals in management jobs had these [leadership] abilities, or competencies, but did not use them at work.

The confusion increased when I often discovered
that the same people did use these competencies in
volunteer work . . . and avocational activities outside of their "main" job. . . . The answer was far
simpler than I thought at first: these people were
choosing not to use their abilities. This was particularly evident in advanced professionals and executives and helped explain the absence of leadership.[27]

So, a final and critical factor in the equation is the individual's level of motivation. This is another juncture where the
pool of potential leaders shrinks. Work experiences and other
developmental opportunities are of limited value if an individual is not inclined to become a leader. Many of us simply do
not want the responsibilities and hardships of leadership. Also,
leaders must often break away from the status quo to lead. Yet
many of us are driven by a need to conform; we fear the risk
of being seen as too unconventional. Psychologist Jane Loevinger
argued that many individuals remain locked at a conformist stage
of personal development.[28] In that stage of development, the
individual has strong needs to conform to group-accepted rules.
Social acceptance and its accompanying sense of belonging are
what make us feel secure. Yet a consistent theme among current conceptions of leadership behavior is the presence of non-
conformist behavior and risk taking—characteristic of James's
twice-borns. Certain family, as well as organizational, environments may be more effective at encouraging risk-taking individuals. In addition, there may be a genetic component (as noted
earlier in the twin studies).

As I mentioned earlier, motivation to lead may be directly
related to self-esteem and power needs. Presumably, people with
strong power needs and high self-esteem would be the most motivated. People with high self-esteem would likely be willing to
try unconventional activities because these individuals do not
need to conform to others' expectations to feel good about themselves. Childhood may be the place where these motives and
feelings are rooted. Instilling them through teaching or training may be difficult.

Beyond the drive provided by these forces, one's stage in life may also be a primary factor in whether an individual is ready to assume a leadership role. We know from the work of psychologist Daniel Levinson that adults pass through a series of life stages during which different needs and motivations arise.[29] How well individuals use the motivations and meet the needs in each phase determines how effective they feel as they move on to the next phase. Richard Boyatzis and David Kolb are currently working on a career phase model that argues that individuals may choose not to use abilities or competencies because they are pursuing a different path.[30] So, for example, consider that an individual who enjoys selling is promoted into a leadership role. Rather than assume the activities associated with leadership, such as establishing direction or motivating the troops, this person continues to find ways to sell. According to Boyatzis and Kolb, this individual has chosen to remain in a particular phase rather than move on to a new one, as required by the leadership role. Significant research, however, has yet to be performed linking leaders to life stages, so these sorts of proposals are still in the realm of speculation.

Implications for Training

We could conclude, then, that the development of leadership ability is a very complex process. It starts before birth, with a prerequisite of certain genes that favor intelligence, physical stamina, and perhaps other qualities. Family members, peers, education, sports, and other childhood experiences then influence the child's need for achievement, power, risk taking, and so on. Work experiences and mentors shape the raw leadership materials of childhood and early adulthood into actual leadership by providing essential knowledge and behavioral skills. Opportunity and luck are the final determinants of who gets a chance to lead. Leaders, then, are a combination of the two schools of thought: they are both born and made. It is quite possible that many people are born with the prerequisites, yet of these, only a few actually go on to become leaders. If this is the case, later life experiences probably determine who the few will be.

If these speculations are correct, what are the implications for training? If experience is such an important teacher, and the motivation to lead is rooted in one's past, and leadership skills are indeed so complex and related to one's work and past, what role can training hope to play? On the surface, it seems a small role, at best. For example, how can we motivate managers to become leaders in a three-day training seminar if a key component — self-esteem — is rooted in childhood? How, in one week, can we teach the ability to envision opportunities in an industry — an ability that seems to require years of experience to develop. How can we teach the interpersonal skills necessary to grasp the needs and unformed aspirations of potential followers when such skills may have a genetic component? It would seem terribly unrealistic to expect such achievements from training, especially when it comes in increments of three to five days.

Yet, I do not feel that pessimism is fully warranted. I am going to put my reputation on the line at this point and say that from my research, I now believe that training can play a vital role in leadership development. Yes, elements of leadership can be taught. But to be successful, training must be designed to (1) develop and refine certain of the teachable skills, (2) improve the conceptual abilities of managers, (3) tap individuals' personal needs, interests, and self-esteem, and (4) help managers see and move beyond their interpersonal blocks. But why these four objectives, in particular?

Let us start with the first one: skills. Presumably, what life experiences are doing is teaching about certain leadership skills and providing knowledge. Work experiences allow individuals to learn, practice, and hone their skills and implement their knowledge. So, for example, a young manager realizes that part of her boss's success is an ability to communicate inspirationally. The young manager practices this skill on appropriate occasions and gradually masters it. On other occasions, she may learn the behaviors that align subordinates in the direction she is proposing. But this describes a largely haphazard process, in the sense that the learning occurs by chance; the occasional good boss or the right job opportunity are crucial. As a result, there is a high probability that certain leadership skills will never be learned or will be only partially developed. Training could formalize this process and ensure that our manager receives exposure to such skills early in her career, rather than allowing chance to be her teacher.

The second training focus, conceptual ability, is twofold. First, leaders often have a strong ability to think conceptually. This plays a vital role in their ability to set direction because the ability to think strategically involves comprehending the current and future environments. Some of this training comes from formal schooling. A significant portion results from native intelligence and industry experience. The rest must come from on-the-job interactions with project teams and co-workers who are thinking through organizational and strategic issues. Again, this ability could be conferred through formal training by exposing junior managers to coursework that encourages conceptual thinking about the issues facing their marketplaces and by giving them conceptual models to use in interpreting information.

A second feature of conceptual ability is the manager's ability to conceptualize the leadership role itself—to understand its distinctiveness from a managerial role, to know how to be and act like a leader. Currently, this is learned largely on the job through observing successful and unsuccessful managers in a company. Training, in this case, could formalize the process by exposing young managers to a rich range of examples of leadership and management in specific company situations and by providing simple models to distinguish between the concepts. Training would essentially build awareness.

Next, personal growth experiences that tap needs and interests and build self-esteem would be important from the perspective of training because each of these components is linked to a leader's own motivation to lead and to formulate a vision. From our earlier discussion, we know that much of the drive and need to be a leader appears to originate in the family. In addition, some of a leader's passionate interests may derive from childhood. Currently, most people's efforts to match their personal interests to their work are quite haphazard; some find opportunities to work on their passions, others do not. In the ideal case, training would help individuals clarify and develop the interests that might help determine their suitability for a particular career.

In addition, leaders must have a good measure of self-esteem in order to appear credible to others and to make courageous, risky decisions. Through confidence-building exercises and formal feedback on an individual's strengths, training might help to build and fortify self-esteem.

Finally, training could stimulate personal growth by heightening a person's awareness of needs that get in the way of leading. For example, ineffective interpersonal behaviors impair a leader's ability to gain commitment from and to motivate followers. By learning effective interpersonal skills, managers could overcome behavioral obstacles to leading.

These primary areas of training — skill building, conceptual development, and personal growth — could play important roles in leadership development. We should also add another — feedback — which is more a learning than a goal area. Knowing where one stands with regard to the other three dimensions requires feedback of some sort. For example, one might ask, "How are my communication skills and in what areas do I need improvement?" Formal feedback procedures ensure that potential leaders clearly and fully understand their strengths and weaknesses. In this way, feedback defines areas for future development.

Interestingly, many of the more innovative programs approach leadership training from just these four perspectives. The question, of course, is whether they succeed in developing leadership abilities.

Chapter Three

From Plato to Peters:
Approaches to
Leadership Training

We should prefer the steadiest and bravest and, so far as
possible, the best looking. But we shall also look not only for moral
integrity and toughness, but for natural aptitude for this kind of
education. . . . They need intellectual eagerness, and must learn
easily. For the mind shirks mental hardship more than physical. . . . They must have good memories, determination, and a
fondness for hard work. . . . If we pick those who are sound in
limb and mind and then put them through our long course of
instruction and training, Justice herself can't blame us and we
shall preserve the constitution of our society.

—Plato

The ancient Greeks were probably not the first people to have
thought about the need to train leaders, but credit for the first
recorded leadership training program does go to Plato, the Greek
philosopher. In *The Republic* he set out his vision for training
leaders for the ideal political state. Starting with good raw material, he felt, was critical to the success of his program. He
clearly leaned toward the belief that genes and childhood are
important determinants of leadership ability. But he also believed that training and work experiences were critical. His candidates, a selection of the "best and brightest," would undergo

rigorous studies of arithmetic and geometry, with a healthy dose of athletics for balance. Afterward came work experience in public office or the military. This was accompanied by in-depth studies in philosophy. Only philosophers, Plato believed, possessed the purity of judgment necessary for the equitable governance of society. Without a solid grounding in this discipline, rulers would fall prey to their own base needs rather than uphold the elevated values of their society. Throughout their many years of preparation, Plato would have tested the candidates to determine which ones should advance to the next level of study and work experience.

Finally, at age fifty — yes, fifty — Plato's candidates would be ready to rule. The individuals who had survived the many tests and trials would serve on a rotating basis: "For the rest of their lives, they will spend the bulk of their time in philosophy, but when their time comes they will, in rotation, turn to the weary business of politics and, for the sake of society, do their duty as Rulers, not for the honour they get by it but as a matter of necessity."[1] As we see, leadership was not something Plato considered rewarding and stimulating. Rather, it was a social necessity; best to find those who could do the job wisely and who would not be seduced by the temptations of power.

Plato's program, however, remained forever an ideal; it was never instituted. Why? Several possible reasons come to mind. First, his program for schooling and training leaders would have required enormous resources and efforts of coordination. Few societies, if any, are prepared to make such an investment. Second, most members of the power structure at the time were not philosophers. Rather, they were men concerned with a very tangible world, many of them driven by needs for achievement and power. They had little interest in creating a system that would replace them with philosophers. After all, to them, politics and governance was a world of action, not reflection. Finally, I suspect that the notion of channeling an elite cadre of individuals from an early age would have been difficult for many to accept (and today, it would probably be seen as a bit totalitarian).

In a curious way, these three perspectives still permeate our view of leadership training today. Most would agree that

to seriously train individuals in the arts of leadership takes enormous time and resources—perhaps more than societies or organizations possess, and certainly more than they are willing
to expend. In organizations, this is seen quite clearly in the constant trade-off between training resources and time: how much
money to spend on something with an uncertain payoff, and
how much time to allow managers to be away from their jobs.

Moreover, those who think about leadership training are
not usually in the power structure. A trainer's concept of what
is necessary to lead may be quite different from an executive's,
just as Plato's belief in philosophers was not widely shared by
the rulers of his time. For example, an executive may have successfully climbed to the top by being highly directive, while a
trainer may see participative approaches as the key to success.
This divergence in perspectives may account for the lack of support for leadership training so often found in upper echelons
of organizations.

Finally, few if any leaders have achieved their positions
because of formal training programs. They see themselves as
having learned from the "school of hard knocks." I am certain
that this belief permeates their own thinking (and the general
population's) when it comes to leadership training. Why would
an organization need to make a formal effort when leadership
is learned by experience and fueled by ambitions? All of these
factors militate against a serious approach to leadership training.

Despite the prevailing belief that the creation of leaders
is an uncontrollable and almost random process, the hope has
persisted that there must be aspects of leadership that surely can
be taught. As a result, since Plato's time numerous "leadership
training programs" have been instituted. More often than not,
these programs have been associated with military training. Ancient and medieval armies, for instance, had various programs
to teach their younger officers the arts of war, with the focus
primarily on physical skills, such as swordmanship. The real
art of leadership, especially strategic leadership, was learned
largely under the tutelage of senior officers during battle. By
the 1700s and 1800s, military academies in Europe and the
United States, however, began to train their cadets formally in

the strategies and tactics of warfare, with the assumption that such knowledge would help them "lead" more effectively in battle.

Yet the military term *leadership* has a somewhat special meaning. As a graduate student, I can recall finding a dusty volume in the library which was a handbook on "leadership development" for soldiers in World War I. As I leafed through the pages, I realized that my idea of leadership did not match the one in this book, which referred to obeying commands from superiors, ensuring that provisions were adequate, maintaining formal reports, disciplining negligent troops, and so on. It was essentially a guide to effective administration in the field. Much of what was termed "leadership training" in the past has been of this nature.

Outside the military, in the spheres of government and religion, "leadership training" has had an equally long history. The ancient Chinese had highly structured training programs to educate bureaucrats in the tenets of Confucianism and other specialized knowledge. Religions such as Catholicism and Buddhism instituted formal programs to educate candidates for future leadership roles in their respective organizations. In both cases, studies centered around church dogma because these "leadership" programs were in reality mechanisms to instill very specialized knowledge into the heads of future administrators. They were conveying information rather than a set of leadership behaviors.

In contrast, the training of leaders for business enterprises has a relatively recent history. The first undergraduate commerce program appeared in 1881 at the Wharton School of the University of Pennsylvania. With the advent of undergraduate programs such as Wharton's and shortly thereafter masters programs (the first Masters of Commercial Science at the Tuck School of Dartmouth College in 1900 and the first Masters in Business Administration at Harvard University in 1908), training for managerial skills began to be taken seriously. At the time, leadership and managership overlapped as concepts, and the distinction we draw today between the two roles was not so sharp. Indeed, the terms were often used interchangeably to name the same set of skills, which could be summarized as functional, strategic, and interpersonal.

Universities concerned themselves largely with the functional and strategic skills, organizing their curriculums around topics such as marketing and strategic management. There were and are courses on interpersonal skills, but a graduate student would typically take only one or two of these over a two-year program. And until very recently, courses devoted solely to the study of leadership were far more likely to be found in political science departments than in management schools.

Leadership training outside of universities most often has occurred "on the job." It was assumed that structured career paths would provide the functional knowledge needed to "lead," so formal hierarchies of positions were designed to provide specialized knowledge and experience and to reward achievement. An example is the product manager system in marketing, where one moves from assistant product manager to associate product manager to product manager. Strategic skills, it was implicitly assumed, were not so important until one reached higher levels in the organization. Once there, these would be learned on the job, with perhaps an occasional outside course.

Interpersonal skills were also to be learned largely on the job, with little attention given to how this would take place other than through random work experiences. Of the three skill areas, however, the interpersonal skills did receive the most attention in terms of outside training. During the 1960s, companies began sending managers off to T-groups at organizations like the National Training Laboratories to help them learn about effective interpersonal behavior.

In addition, there have been and are the "situational leadership" programs, such as those developed by Paul Hersey, of the University of Massachusetts, and Kenneth Blanchard, author of *The One Minute Manager*. By the 1960s and 1970s, programs like theirs had become the standard for leadership training in companies. Typically, such programs have been built around a contingency theory of leader effectiveness, using the two leadership roles identified by researchers at Ohio State and the University of Michigan, task and relationship. Proponents of these programs assert that if leaders are to be successful, their styles need to be appropriate to the situation (the situation being the leader, followers, superiors, associates, job and organizational demands) and the maturity of their group members (ability and willingness of people to take responsibility for directing their own behavior). Therefore, in certain situations, they need to be more task oriented; in other situations, more people oriented.

Training begins with the administration of the Leadership Effectiveness and Adaptability Description (LEAD) instrument. This assessment describes twelve situations and four possible leadership actions for each situation. Respondents are asked to choose the action they feel best represents their leadership style. This self-diagnosis is the starting point for helping participants enlarge their repertoire of leadership behaviors. They come to see their strengths and weaknesses as leaders along these dimensions. From there, role-playing and skill-building exercises expose participants to the "ideal" responses to each situation and provide opportunities for them to improve their weaker skills.[2]

This type of program was typical ten to fifteen years ago: a model was proposed, a diagnostic instrument was used to orient participants, and then skill-building exercises were done that were derived from a "task versus relationship" contingency model. While these programs continue to be popular, today they are more accurately classified as managerial or supervisory leadership training programs because they put little emphasis on the skills of strategic envisioning, inspirational speaking, or on managing significant organizational change.

With the advent of the 1980s, however, several important developments took place in leadership training. Training moved beyond the simpler task versus social dimensions of "leading" to expanded conceptions of the leader as change agent, visionary, and motivator. So, for example, the role of strategic vision in leadership suddenly became particularly important in training—in response to the intensifying competitive pressures of the times.

In addition, the 1980s brought greater experimentation with learning methods. Specifically, action learning (in which participants learned by using actual company issues), which was pioneered some thirty years ago in Great Britain by Reginald

Revens, caught on as companies like General Electric began using actual strategic issues as leadership training problems for their senior managers.

Particularly significant, however, were in-house executive-level company experiments that linked corporate education in leadership to changing company strategy and culture. Previously, leadership education had been largely reserved for supervisors and midlevel managers. (Senior managers often joined university programs such as Harvard's Advanced Management Program, though the emphasis was primarily on general management skills such as strategy formulation rather than on leadership per se.) Corporations such as Federated Department Stores, General Foods, Motorola, and Xerox developed programs for their executives that attempted to instill the notion of the leader as an implementor of change and molder of corporate culture.[3] So, for example, in 1983, the then-president and chief executive officer (CEO) of General Foods, Philip Smith, sponsored the Business Leadership Program. In small groups, the top four hundred executives examined their strategic visions for their divisions and for the company, assessed their own leadership strengths and weaknesses, and designed personal action plans to implement their learnings.[4]

There were other experiments as well. For example, the Square D Company, an electrical products manufacturer in Palatine, Illinois, established a Vision College, a two-day course on the company's goals and philosophies on customer service, quality, and growth, wherein leadership themes were woven throughout. Eventually, more than 75 percent of the company's almost twenty thousand employees would graduate from the college. Levi-Strauss, the jeans maker, not only undertook similar companywide training of many of its employees but also began experiments with "back home" devices to encourage and reward leadership through special performance appraisals and company forums. Both companies' efforts were attempts to socialize employees into a mind-set of leadership.

At the same time, a handful of academic institutions, such as the University of Chicago, the Wharton School, and the University of Virginia, began interesting experiments with innovative leadership coursework. For example, today MBA candidates at the University of Virginia, at the beginning of their second year, participate in a six-day executive-style seminar, the introductory component of a required course called Leadership. They spend the six days discussing the key competencies of leadership, team building in outdoor-adventure exercises, and working on a management simulation game. The Leadership course includes case discussion classes, team consulting assignments provided by international companies, and a week of data gathering in Europe by the students, who deliver written and oral presentations to the sponsoring companies. As leadership continues to attract the attention of the business press, we can expect to see more graduate business schools entering the field of leadership education with programs like Virginia's.

While academic leadership programs are beginning to proliferate, many of the company experiments mentioned earlier have had short lifetimes; sometimes they have fallen victim to mergers or new CEOs, and other programs were never seen as more than "one shot" efforts. In-house experiments continue at places like General Electric and Levi-Strauss, but only a handful of other companies have tried large-scale, integrative efforts at leadership development. Instead, corporations have come to rely almost entirely on outside vendors for leadership training programs. Consequently, outside programs are important proving grounds for leadership education at present, and for this reason, they were chosen as the focus of our investigation.

Leadership Training Programs in the 1990s

As noted, innovation in leadership training in the last several years has come mainly from independent training organizations. To date, there have been no formal attempts at investigating these programs, only scattered in-company evaluations. What they do, what their objectives are, and what participants can learn from them are unanswered questions.

Each of the five programs I explore in this book emphasizes one of these four categories of leadership training, noted at the end of Chapter Two: personal growth, conceptual understanding, feedback, and skill building. None of the five, however, presents all four areas with equal emphasis. Instead, one approach dominates significantly in each program; for example, a program geared toward a conceptual understanding of leadership may employ skill-building exercises and feedback instruments, but its dominant orientation is conceptual.

An aspect of all five leadership training programs that surprised me and that I want to emphasize is that each program reflects the background of its principal designer or founder. For example, several course designers from the Leadership Challenge and the Center for Creative Leadership are former Peace Corps members. In both courses we find a strong emphasis on the "helping" and "empowering" leader—a similar orientation to that of the Peace Corps, whose members work to help and empower Third World peoples. Other programs were founded by academics, and these tend to be oriented strongly toward research-based paradigms. Thus, one clue to a program's orientation is the background and pedagogical training of its founder.

In addition, I discovered that all five of the programs I studied were still evolving. All were continuing to experiment with new materials and new exercises when I or my research assistant participated in them. This experimentation is indicative of the state of continual change in the field. While change makes for exciting times in leadership training, it makes it difficult for users to discriminate between methods that are effective and those that are not.

From these general observations, we can now turn to a brief overview of each approach. We begin our orientation with the personal growth programs, since these have been generating some of the greatest interest as well as the greatest controversy.

Leadership Training Through Personal Growth

Leadership training programs that emphasize personal growth emerged in the 1980s. They are based, generally, on the assumption that leaders are individuals who are deeply in touch with their personal dreams and talents and who will act to fulfill

them. Profoundly influenced by the ideas of the humanistic psychologies of the 1960s and the 1970s, these programs argue that
most managers are ignoring an inner call to realize their potential
to become leaders. If they could get in touch with their innermost desires and abilities, more managers could transform themselves into leaders. This is an intriguing notion — but one which,
as we shall see, may have been too simplistic in its conceptuali-
zation of leadership.

Using outdoor-adventure activities and psychological exercises, personal growth programs induce participants to reflect
on their behaviors (such as their orientation toward risk or personal intimacy) and on their personal values and desires. They
also empower participants through experiences that teach them
to take responsibility for their situations — rather than blame
problems on the job on outside influences or events.

In this book, we will examine two of the better known
programs: Pecos River Learning Center and ARC International.
In the concluding chapter, we will also look at a third and newer
program, LeaderLab, developed by the Center for Creative
Leadership. The first program, Pecos River, was founded by
Larry Wilson. Wilson began his career in sales, selling life insurance, at age twenty-three. By twenty-nine, he had become
the youngest lifetime member of the life insurance industry's
prestigious Million Dollar Round Table. From there, he went
on to become a popular speaker and consultant for major corporations on the art of selling. He became so successful that in
1965 he decided to found his own company, the Wilson Learning Corporation, to market his ideas about effective sales techniques. Sales figures for Wilson Learning eventually grew to
some $60 million. In 1982, however, Wilson decided to sell the
company and begin a new venture, the Pecos River Learning
Center, near Santa Fe, New Mexico. His idea was to merge
outdoor adventure, indoor experiential exercises focusing on personal growth, and lectures on change theories into an educational experience to improve individuals' organizational effectiveness.

Set in a somewhat remote area of New Mexico, the program operates out of a 1,700-acre ranch between the Rocky

Mountains and the Sangre de Cristo range—a spectacular setting. Though we will explore the program's objectives in depth later, it could be said that risk taking and teamwork are two principal aims of the program.

ARC International is the offshoot of a business training organization created in Japan by Robert White. White, like Wilson, had been involved in sales training and personal growth experiences early in his career. He served as president of two of the pioneer personal growth seminars, Mind Dynamics, Inc., and Lifespring, Inc. In 1974, he began marketing American Salesmasters sales and management training programs in Japan. His successes there led to the expansion of his enterprise in Japan to include other seminars, such as Life Dynamics (personal effectiveness training seminars), the Kyudo System of project planning and time management training, and the Making of a Salesman training program. By the late 1980s, ARC's sales had grown to approximately $35 million and employees numbered some 150 worldwide.

White's considerable experience with the human potential movement had included his involvement with Lifespring. He counted Werner Erhard among his friends. White's strong personal growth orientation is captured in a comment he made to me: "Our aim is to help others treat each other as human beings and make organizations a wonderful place to be and work in." This quotation from ARC literature further illustrates their human potential orientation: "Our work at ARC International is characterized by attending to this unique power in human beings. We believe that latent in every person [are] enormous untapped resources, and that this resourcefulness is released primarily by recognizing that it is there. Our work is designed to enable individuals, groups, and organizations to tap into this powerful resource in order to become more creative and more effective in achieving their aims—to live more effectively in this world of possibility. If we were to sum up our work in one sentence, it would probably be this: Our work is designed to help people take responsibility in their work and in their lives."

In this last statement, we see the core philosophy behind these types of programs: to take responsibility for one's life. ARC is an acronym for "Creating Results through *A*wareness, *Re*-sponsibility, and *C*ommunication," and the VisionQuest program (which I participated in) is built around a series of largely experiential exercises designed to encourage personal reflection and accountability and ultimately the formulation of a personally meaningful vision.

Leadership Development Through Conceptual Understanding

Training in the conceptual understanding of leadership has traditionally been the domain of the universities. Theory oriented by nature, graduate and undergraduate programs have focused on the issue of leadership development through a cognitive understanding of the phenomenon. Models and case studies have been used to explain to students and managers what leaders actually do. While there is usually a humanistic orientation (such as teaching the value of Theory Y, teamwork, and participation in such programs), there is often a greater realism in their content than, say, compared to the personal growth programs. For example, university students are taught contingency models of leadership that demonstrate that participation is not always appropriate, whereas personal growth programs emphasize participation as a more universal practice. The lecture–case–discussion format, however, provides few or no opportunities for students to reflect deeply on their own desires to become leaders or to test out their leadership abilities. Skill building in these settings is limited because the pedagogical tools are often lectures and discussions, rather than experiential exercises.

Beyond university settings, there are several commercial leadership development programs whose orientations are strongly conceptual. For example, they distinguish between the concepts of leadership and managership. These programs, usually built around a single model of leadership, employ supporting skill-building and feedback material. Because they must serve the marketplace, they do not simply teach concepts but also train participants in the competencies related to the concepts. The conceptual program we chose to investigate is The Leadership

Challenge program, developed by James Kouzes and Barry Posner, and offered through the company of management consultant Tom Peters and his TPG/Learning Systems. Kouzes and Posner's workshop was developed out of a research project that resulted in a book entitled *The Leadership Challenge: How to Get Extraordinary Things Done in Organizations,* published in 1987 by Jossey-Bass. Kouzes and Posner focused their research on observations of what leaders did to encourage extraordinary accomplishments.

Five sets of behavior are distinguished, which constitute the core of a four-day public workshop and a variety of in-company seminars. While the program contains skill-building experiences and feedback, it introduces participants to the ideas behind Kouzes and Posner's leadership research. Its aim is to stimulate participants to think deeply about leadership and to have initial experiences of the behaviors associated with leading.

Conceptual programs, such as The Leadership Challenge, are a natural first step when our understanding of something undergoes a significant change. This is especially pertinent here, given the complexity of the leadership behaviors introduced in the models of the 1980s. Harvard Business School professor John Kotter's comments to me expand on this perspective: "Most leadership skills are either too complex to train or else too poorly understood to be trainable. The skills needed in big jobs are sometimes much more complicated than are taught in leadership courses. The best we can do with training is to provide a catalyst to catch managers' attention to some important skill areas. The key is not to really develop the skills in the classroom, but to help managers appreciate them and gain awareness. The value of this aspect of leadership training is in helping people to understand what leadership really is. This awareness building can also stimulate participants' enthusiasm about the idea of leading." Conceptual training, then, serves the function of expanding participants' perceptions of the process and of what it requires as well as generating interest in becoming a leader. Ultimately, however, the responsibility still rests with the individual and his or her organization to create leadership experiences afterward.

Leadership Development Through Feedback

Leadership training can be approached from the perspective that most of us already possess leadership skills in varying degrees and strengths. In some of us, these may be more latent than apparent. Through effective feedback processes, we can learn about our strengths and weaknesses in a number of leadership skills. The next logical step is to develop the weaker skills or to acquire the absent skills while continuing to emphasize our stronger ones. Programs in which feedback is emphasized tend to be method driven (for example, feedback and experiential exercises are learning methods), whereas the other approaches are concerned with distinct outcomes produced by learning methods such as personal growth.

Most leadership programs employ some form of feedback to participants. Some use peer feedback, such as ARC's personal growth programs, where participants in small groups describe how their personalities affect each other. Others may use feedback instruments. For example, The Leadership Challenge uses a feedback instrument built around the program's model of the five steps in leading others.

In a few programs, however, feedback constitutes a large portion of the session time and measures participants' skills in a wide range of behaviors. The program that exemplifies this approach is the Leadership Development Program offered by the Center for Creative Leadership in North Carolina. While this six-day leadership program involves experiential exercises and some conceptual material, its predominant feature is feedback.

For example, before arriving at the program, participants fill out extensive feedback instruments as varied as the Myers-Briggs Type Indicator, the Firo-B, and the Management Skills Profile, along with other instruments designed by the Center. These instruments are also given to the participants' peers, bosses, and subordinates to assess the individual. Throughout the six days, participants receive bits and pieces of feedback, until the fifth day, which is devoted entirely to staff and peer feedback. Armed with information on an array of dimensions, participants return home with insights into how their behavior affects themselves and others. It is assumed that after the program, participants will have the personal motivation to improve.

Leadership Development Through Skill Building

Skill building is the most commonly employed methodology in management training, yet we find relatively few effective versions of these programs treating the newer conceptions of leadership. Earlier models of leadership training lent themselves fairly easily to skill-building formats. For instance, the task and social dimensions of leadership were essentially derived from concrete behavior observed in groups and so could easily be presented as skills people could learn. Newer conceptions of leadership involve much more complex skills, especially cognitive and psychological skills, which are difficult to teach. For example, the processes of strategic visioning and assessing follower needs are known to involve a significance base of experience. Neither skill lends itself to development over a five-day training experience.

Nonetheless, programs do exist that attempt to teach many of these complex behaviors. One of these is the Forum Company of Boston (no relation to Werner Erhard's Forum). As well, management professors Bernard Bass and Bruce Avolio, at the State University of New York at Binghamton, have developed a program for transformational leadership skills, based on their research.

The approach of these skill-building programs is relatively straightforward. Program designers identify what they perceive to be the key leadership skills that can be taught. These are formulated into modules and introduced to participants. For example, the Forum Company identifies four steps in effective leading: (1) interpreting (the environment), (2) shaping (the vision), (3) mobilizing (employees to achieve the vision), and (4) inspiring (employees to accomplish the vision). Under each general category are a set of behavioral skills. During the module on inspiring, for instance, participants first complete an exercise where they consider situations in which their work was affected by the presence or absence of inspiration. They identify the actual techniques or practices that inspired them. The instructor describes additional, similar practices. A case study is used to illustrate the effective or ineffective use of these practices. With an understanding of the skill clearly in mind, participants practice performing this particular skill by giving inspirational talks. Their performance is critiqued, and feedback directs them to their stronger and weaker points. Presumably after the seminar, they continue to practice and refine their skills.

These programs tend to be most popular for training at the supervisory or midmanagement level. Training organizations are able to simplify the leadership skills for these levels, thus turning complex skills into teachable ones. For example, the Zenger-Miller training company offers a Frontline Leadership program for supervisors. They teach behavior modeling using videotapes of realistic examples, discussion, practice, feedback, and planning activities that utilize skills. At last report, their Frontline program comprised nineteen skill areas grouped into five clusters, each cluster corresponding to a specific job function of the manager, such as developing team performance, managing change and innovation, or communicating (interpersonal skills). Each skill is relatively straightforward; the more complex, less easily taught skills associated with leadership at senior organizational levels are not covered.

In theory, all leadership training programs should have a skill-building component—if indeed leadership can be taught—but many programs have only a limited emphasis. However, I believe this reflects the fact that many of the skills that we recognize today as pertaining to leadership may be too complex to teach. We will return to this issue later.

Do Any Programs Actually Develop Leaders?

I have presented the four approaches to leadership training that we will examine in the five programs described in this book. At this point, you might be asking yourself whether any of these approaches alone is sufficient to induce leadership qualities. One concern you might have is that each approach appears to offer only one of the pieces that would seem to be necessary to complete the puzzle of leadership development. In other words, leadership development in the ideal case should incorporate experiences in personal growth, conceptual understanding, skill building, and feedback. Instead, one approach may dominate at the cost of the others.

This issue will be discussed in greater depth in Chapter

Eight, but for now it is sufficient to say that this assumption is largely correct. The ideal program would begin with a conceptual overview, then provide feedback on where participants stand relative to the skills associated with the conceptual model of leadership. This would be followed by skill building, for skills that are teachable. The skills that are more complex (and therefore less amenable to being taught) would be the focus of awareness building, with the idea that participants could find long-term opportunities to develop these skills back at the office. Feedback would reappear after preliminary skill building to assess how well individuals have learned and understood the skills, and this would be followed by more skill building. Personal growth experiences would be used along the way as powerful opportunities for reflection on two levels: to help managers determine their own desires to lead, and to free participants of ineffective behaviors. This, of course, would be the ideal.[5] Some programs come close, but a balanced version of this plan does not exist, because, I would argue, program designers are caught to some extent in their own paradigms of pedagogy. As a result, most programs are oriented strongly toward one of the four approaches. Just as important (and no fault of the designers), programs are too short to have a more lasting impact, especially in terms of developing many skills.

In any program, there should be elements of artistry, adventure, and personal risk taking—but sometimes these are missing. I am convinced that one reason the personal growth programs are so memorable is that they offer many "up-ending experiences." Programs that provide a challenging "rite of passage" have an enormous symbolic advantage over other more mundane educational experiences. This element must somehow be incorporated into all training experiences.

Having laid some initial groundwork, let us now turn to each of the four approaches to leadership training to assess their unique contributions and their unique drawbacks from a participant's viewpoint. The next four chapters record the personal experiences of either myself or my research assistant Ann Latimer. You will join us as we experience the ups and downs of each program. Our adventure starts with the personal growth approaches.

Part Two

The Diary of a Trainee

Chapter Four

Finding My True Self: The Personal Growth Approaches

*H*umans no longer have instincts in the animal sense, powerful, unmistakable inner voices which tell them unequivocally what to do, when, where, how and with whom. All that we have left are instinct-remnants. And furthermore, these are weak, subtle, and delicate, very easily drowned out by learning, by cultural expectations, by fear, by disapproval, etc. They are hard to know, rather than easy. Authentic self-hood can be defined in part as being able to hear these impulse voices within oneself, i.e., to know what one really wants or doesn't want, what one is fit for and what one is not fit for.

—Abraham Maslow

At the heart of the personal growth programs is Abraham Maslow's idea of finding what your true self is and wants — and perhaps in that process discovering your ability to lead. The steps that the personal growth programs offer to arrive at this point of enlightenment range from jumping off cliffs to intense personal explorations with others. The Pecos River Learning Center and ARC's VisionQuest are our stops on this particular track of leadership training. We begin with the Pecos River program.

Epigraph from *Toward a Psychology of Being* by Abraham Maslow. Copyright © 1968 by Van Nostrand Reinhold. Reprinted with permission.

Pecos River: "Between Two Trapezes"

To understand Pecos River, one needs to understand the character of its founder, Larry Wilson. Like many New Age organizations, this one reflects the charismatic leader who stands behind it. Wilson's former career in sales is evident in the energy and enthusiasm he exudes for his Pecos River Learning Center in Santa Fe, New Mexico. With monies from the sale of his previous enterprise, Wilson Learning, Wilson transformed arid ranch land into a management training center, complete with hotel, hot tubs, gourmet restaurant, and tennis courts.

When asked in a recent interview to describe his goals for the Pecos River Learning Center, Wilson commented, "People change in three different ways. The first is through shock. You get a divorce, you lose your job, you have a heart attack. The shock wakes you up. Another way that people change is through evolution. You look around and see everyone else is changing and think that maybe you can do it, too. We call that adapting. There are costs connected with both these kinds of change. The cost of a heart attack is obvious, and the cost of an evolutionary change is the amount of opportunity lost. The third way people change is through anticipation. You go out, take a look around, create a vision, come back, decide that something is different than it is. That's the creative or strategic process. What we try to do here is give people a little bit of all three ways to learn — a little bit of crisis, a lot of support and evolution and, with companies especially, a lot of the creative process."

Pecos River is an adventure-based, experiential learning program that, as Wilson describes it, makes you feel "between two trapezes." In other words, it attempts to create a state where you are letting go of one stage in your life to start another. Much of the program focuses on the idea of anticipation and on risk taking and teamwork. For individuals, its focus is primarily on personal growth. For company groups, there is a greater emphasis on teamwork and on addressing specific organizational issues. The techniques are, as one journalist remarked, "a salad of borrowings from philosophers, futurists, physicists, psychologists, and business leaders, seasoned by Wilson's own experience."[1]

Risk taking is a favorite theme of the Pecos River program and much of it takes place in the outdoor adventure facility. But risk taking is also practiced on an interpersonal level through a series of exercises that allow participants to practice intimate sharing, disclose their feelings, request support, and look foolish. The idea of all these exercises is to push individuals past their personal safety boundaries. Behind these experiences is the assumption that leaders are individuals who possess the self-confidence to take risks, and so risk taking becomes a central focus of the program.

A typical program at the Pecos River Learning Center unfolds as follows. There are essentially three parts. The initial sessions lay the groundwork for the course by introducing basic models of how individuals and organizations change. There is an examination of forces that impede change, with particular emphasis on the forces within individuals. The second part involves outdoor activities. Here participants are faced with the issues of risk taking, teamwork, and being supportive. The final sessions focus on achieving greater personal intimacy and a personal vision. (Programs for corporations will vary somewhat from this model, with more attention going to such specific issues as strategy, organizational change, and teamwork.)

The first day is spent orienting participants to what lies ahead. Larry Wilson, or another individual, opens the orientation. The morning is devoted to loosening participants up in terms of becoming more risk oriented and letting down their inhibitions around self-expression. This is accomplished through what one journalist aptly called "organized silliness." The Pecos River Learning Center has a staff member whose sole job is to be what the French call an "animateur." This individual is the entertainer. He asks participants to do silly warm-ups. (A hallmark of the program is that staff members assume very clear roles. We know who will speak to us about the more serious aspects and who will tease and prod us into play.) Our animateur's first job is introductions. We are asked to find someone who has the same thumb size and, afterward, someone who uses the same toothpaste. As we pursue these quests, we introduce ourselves and talk about why we are attending the program.

Later, we will be asked to pretend that we have been invited to audition for the Santa Fe ballet and to dance the ballet
as beautifully as possible. Then we pretend to audition for the
Santa Fe opera and sing as magnificently as possible. These and
other exercises are geared to release our inhibitions and in many
ways are important first steps in preparing participants psychologically to share on a more personal level later in the course.

On the first day, also, we are introduced to the models
that the course will use. These center around change processes
for individuals and organizations. Paraphrasing from George
Land's *Grow or Die,* Wilson explains:

> In the biology model of growth, there are three
> phases. Phase I is formative. It's the beginning. It's
> a period of trial and error. If you're starting a new
> company, this is an entrepreneurial period. If you're
> starting a new relationship, this is when you look
> for ways to connect. You're looking for roles. The
> goal of Phase I is to get to a replicatable process.
>
> Phase II is normative. Here we are looking
> for new ideas only if they support the replicatable
> process we found in Phase I. In Phase II we create
> boundaries. We decide what we aren't going to be
> as well as what we are going to be. An operating
> principle of Phase II is "If it ain't broke, don't fix
> it." Another principle, especially of late Phase II,
> is "nothing fails like success." One characteristic of
> late Phase II in business is arrogance. We know
> what the customer needs.
>
> When Phase II begins to go wrong, we say
> you hit the wall. Profits are down; market share
> is down. This is where transformation begins. This
> is where you must get over the wall to begin Phase
> III.
>
> Most of American industry today is in the
> process of hitting the wall. Whatever got them there
> is what they must let go of. In nature, this process
> is called bifurcation. It's a new beginning, such as

occurs in hybridization. The best of the old combines with the new to produce something entirely different. In nature, it's a supportive process. In business, it's not. The organizational immunization system wants to kill anything new. The creative process is in jeopardy at this point. Managing this kind of transition is a huge problem today.

An operating principle of Phase III is that we don't have the answers. As we move into the new era, we are asking people to think. It's only when people face crisis or shock, or know that they don't know, that change is possible.[2]

This is the rationale for the course—we are entering Phase III. From here, we go into a discussion of the importance of vision, a subject to which we will return later in the week. Also presented is a personal change model involving the three main means of changing: shock, evolution, and anticipation. Briefly summarized, shock is change through a crisis of some sort—a heart attack, being fired from a job, or midlife crisis. These incidents demand change within the person. Evolution involves seeing others changing and then evolving with them. Anticipation is foreseeing the need for change and acting in advance— being visionary in one's change.

In many ways, the program embodies change along these three pathways. Shock comes in the form of risks taken in the outdoor-adventure activities. Evolution comes in the form of seeing other participants succeeding in various events and realizing that you, too, can do it. Anticipation is accomplished through a personal vision exercise toward the end of the program.

Two other important ideas are introduced early on. The first is the role of the ego in defending our worldview and in providing obstacles to learning. At one point, Wilson unveils a seven-foot green dragon standing in one corner of the seminar room. The dragon, Wilson explains, is the symbol for our ego's defenses. It will do anything to protect the hidden treasure within us—the ego. To learn, we must be able to say no to the ego, to override its fears. "Most of us spend 30 to 40 percent of our energy resource defending ourselves, guarding ourselves, trying to be cool, trying to protect an image," Wilson tells us. The dragon proved to be a very helpful image and metaphor for many participants. I, for example, found myself constantly reminded of it whenever I faced risks in the program. (The capturing of important ideas in simple symbols is a little-utilized technique, but, I believe, a vital part of an effective training program.)

The second important idea, Wilson explains, is contained in an acronym: TASTE. "Our goal for the weekend is to experience 100 percent truth, accountability, support, trust, and energy — or TASTE. . . . Truth and accountability will come in the personal risk experiences. Support and trust during the ropes course. Energy will come from doing each of the others 100 percent." These, then, become the goals for the program.

With these models and ideas in place, we embark on the second phase of the course, the outdoor adventures. From the participants' perspective, this is the part of the course that has the greatest personal impact. It embodies most powerfully the themes of teamwork and risk taking. I have excerpted Patricia Galagan's description of the experience because I feel she has captured it quite reliably in terms of the process and the emotions that one experiences:

The Pole

All day we've been trying out degrees of physical risk with the help of a supportive partner or team. We begin with a simple trust fall, taking turns falling a few inches back onto the upheld hands of a partner. Next, one by one, we climb onto an adobe wall that is about five feet high, and fall backward into a blanket of hands held up by our huddled teammates, or spotters, as they are called. The call "spotters ready" will ring out all weekend as a signal that a group is ready to support someone's risk taking.

A blind trust walk, in which one partner is blindfolded and led around the ranch by a partner who can see but who may not speak, teaches us how easy or difficult it is to trust one's safety to another person. Then we switch roles, and some people find it is even harder to be responsible for someone else. In the processing that follows, people realize that in addition to experiencing giving and getting trust, they had to learn how to communicate without speaking.

A picnic lunch gives us a break before the first rope event: a relatively simple walk, with a partner, along a wire, with a cluster of spotters ready to restore balance. Again, to succeed you must work with your partner and communicate your intentions.

It helps to think of the ropes course as a playground outside your normal level of risk taking. The exercises are mainly about giving and getting support to take the risk and about turning fear into productive energy. How do you do this? "Live the fear," says Phil Bryson.

Fear is waiting at The Pole. Our team, the Phoenixes, walks across a mountain meadow and down a dirt track toward the Pecos River on whose edge stands the pole and trapeze in a stand of riotously yellow aspen trees. There is a ladder against the lower half of the pole and a series of slats nailed to it at intervals to the top. We can just barely see the small wooden disk onto which we must climb and then stand without any support. The trapeze toward which we are to jump hangs about twelve feet from the top of the pole.

Richard Schaffe, in charge of the event, shows us the helmets, harnesses, and safety lines we will wear, but also lets us know that the wooden disk is not stable and the pole may begin to whiplash.

When you must climb it, a twenty-five foot pole looks as tall as the Washington Monument.

Deborah, the rashest or bravest Phoenix, scrambles into a harness and sprints up the pole while the rest of us are still gaping in disbelief at what we must do. Deborah stands up on the disk, turns 180 degrees as neatly as a ballet dancer, and leaps out to catch the trapeze. Rich and two other belayers let her down on her safety lines amid our astonished cheers.

But Deborah's bravado is not typical. Most of us find a wall of fear somewhere between the top of the ladder and the leap. Gail Larsen, who, in her life on the ground is a poised public speaker and former association top executive, encounters several walls. First her left foot refuses to leave the top rung on the pole and join her right foot on the small wooden disk. Then she is unable to let go of the disk with her hands and stand up straight. Rich coaches her, the Phoenixes cheer her on, unable to look away as she meets and surmounts each challenge. As she turns toward the trapeze, the pole begins to shake and with it her legs. Rich assures her she has balance even though her legs, the disk, and the pole are all in motion. Just when it seems she must fall, she regains control. Finally, she bolts for the trapeze and our collective hurrah releases as much tension as it conveys our joy. Our necks ache from craning upward, but no one minds. We are cheering her determination and her success, which clearly is ours, too.

All fifteen of the Phoenixes, who range in age from early twenties to mid-sixties, try the pole. Even the most height fearing manage to get close to the top rung. What prods most of us is the group's support and the realization that we are perfectly safe. Even if you fall off the pole or the disk, or miss the trapeze, as I did, your safety lines keep you from bodily harm. The risk you imagine is much greater than the real risk, and understanding and controlling this imagined peril is the heart of what the pole teaches. You're left with the ability to concentrate on making decisions about what action to take next and on what you are feeling at each moment. Each move gives you immediate feedback, from yourself, from the facilitator, and from your team holding you in their rapt concentration.

Later, going over the experience with our group, it is clear that the self-consciousness of day one is gone. We are noticeably more receptive to each other. This feeling of trust will be critical in the interpersonal exercises ahead. We learn that though there were many approaches to the challenges of the pole, the lessons came from being as much as possible in the experience. In retrospect, I appreciated how Rich, the facilitator, helped us internalize feelings of control and competence. Often he would ask, "What would it take to make you feel that you've mastered this event?"

The Big Zip

High on the exhilaration of seeing every single Phoenix up and off the pole, we practically run to the next event — the zip wire. Even as we scramble into harnesses and helmets, we are checking out the pitch and length of the wire that stretches across the Pecos River and up to a cliff eighty-five feet above us.

To cross the river, we must use a bridge made of three hairy yellow nylon ropes stretched in a deep V across the water. "The best way to do this," says Phil Bryson, "is to squat down a little bit, hold the ropes apart, and keep your eyes on the opposite bank." Though the rope bridge swoops and quivers, and the single line on which we walk seems impossibly small and the current terribly swift below, we charge across as if invincible. Then up a steep rocky trail, dodging cactus thorns, to the big rock from which the 125-foot zip wire descends.

Phil climbs up with us. Two helpers are already on the rock to man the lines that bring the slide and handles back up to the top after each trip. More helpers are visible below, mere specks at the other end of the wire. Phil hooks each person onto a safety line, and we sit in single file, like parachutists about to leave the plane.

When it is your turn, Phil transfers your safety line from the rock to the zip wire apparatus — a pair of handles and wheels that will take you down the wire. You step up to the edge of the cliff and plant your toes in the void. You look down into the abyss into which you are expected, momentarily, to jump. Phil, at your side, his hand on your shoulder, reminds you to be aware of what is around you. With difficulty, you pull your mind back to the river curving through the valley, the panorama of mountains catching the setting sun, the still bright sky and pink-streaked clouds. Phil checks and double checks your safety line and tells you how to depart the cliff: "Push the handles out and jump off after them."

You know exactly how it goes, having seen ten other people plunge off the rock into a deep parabolic curve that levels out for the swift flight across the river into the waiting arms of your teammates at the bottom. You have the whole terrifying video clearly in your head. So it is time to decide. I will turn my fear, in this case of the first big drop into space, into exhilaration. I will deliberately change the way I view the act I am about to commit.

Taking a deep breath and a firm grip on the handles, I look down past my feet already partly off the rock's edge, out across the rushing river to the valley dotted with shimmering gold aspens, to the cliffs on the other side of the rosy clouds massed above them. I check the whole horizon, absorb the immensity and beauty of what is before me, and leap into it.

The plunge is over before it registers, and I'm already into the quick sliding curve, soaring over the river. People are cheering above and below me. I want to flap the wings I'm sure I must have, but more prudently, I swing my legs to be part of the force and the motion, dancing myself down to my cheering, beaming teammates.

"Your face has changed," a woman tells me, and from the way I feel, I'm sure it has.

That night, during and after dinner, we process. Everyone is in a mood to climb Everest. [From *Training & Development Journal.* Copyright © March 1987, the American Society for Training and Development. Reprinted with permission. All rights reserved.]

The important question is the extent to which such dramatic experiences are transferable. If one thinks about the contexts of outdoor adventures and office environments, it is easy to see that there are few similarities. It is, indeed, a bold leap to argue that there should be any crossover. Jumping off a cliff is a far more immediate and intense experience than making a decision to invest five hundred thousand dollars into a new product's development. In addition, the risk with the cliff is minimal (though oftentimes the conscious mind does not realize this), since individuals have lots of safety devices to protect them. A bad product investment, however, might cause a manager great personal harm in terms of career development. Though with the latter, the decision, and therefore the risk, is usually shared among many managers, and there is also an illusion of objectivity after market share reports and other data are analyzed to justify the project. But otherwise, there are few similarities. So is there any real value to these experiences?

Based on my own personal experiences and those of other participants, I believe there is some carryover. The experience remains in the mind as a metaphor, as a vivid reminder to remain open to risk taking. I will speak from personal experience. As I mentioned earlier, I had just been promoted with tenure at my university when I participated in the Pecos River program. While in many ways, the promotion was a blessing—after all, lifetime job security is nothing to be laughed at—I nonetheless was concerned about the prospect of all that security. I felt that my teaching and my classroom creativity might plateau. Jumping off that cliff was both a frightening and a confidence-building experience for me. In accomplishing it, I internalized it as a metaphor for taking more risks in my life. The year that followed was my most creative year in the classroom. I reminded myself of my courage in jumping off the cliff when I felt hesitant about taking risks in my classroom. But the issue is perhaps more complicated. Was the Pecos River program the only or the primary catalyst? No, in reality, receiving tenure lay the groundwork for my dissatisfaction with the status quo. Tenure had given me the security to take risks knowing that only under unusual circumstances could I be fired by the university. So, paradoxically, I had the security and support to take those risks—something that not having tenure could not have provided. Although I perceived it as providing too much security, tenure, in reality, became my safety line when I "jumped off" into career risks. Organizations would have to provide similar safety lines for managers who returned to work after the program.

In the third section of the Pecos River program, participants move from the literal risk of jumping off a cliff to the risk of opening up to other people. This involves trusting other people with important personal information and believing that they will suspend judgment of you. In a series of sharing exercises, participants experience personal disclosure. For example, we are asked to think of a participant to be our partner—"someone who will stretch you while you share an intense personal experience." Our facilitator instructs us, "Who would be the ideal person for you to be with in this intense emotional experience? Choose someone who you believe will help you go all the way you can. Look around the room. Write the name of that person down on a card and put the card in your pocket. Now, in a few sec-

onds, you can communicate. Now I want you to go to the partner you picked. Everyone up, and find your partner."

We all jump up and begin searching for our partners. In-
evitably, the partner I wanted had chosen someone else, and
several individuals who had chosen me discovered that I was
not searching for them. There is chaos in the room. Then we
hear a command to sit down with our partners. I settle on a
partner whom I did not pick but whom I like and would probably have put second or third on my list.

Larry Wilson calls out, "The game's over!" We are all a
little surprised because we are assuming the exercise has just
begun. Now we find out that it is all over. Wilson asks how many
of us are with the partner we had chosen. Out of sixty-some
participants, perhaps six hands go up. He asks us, "Why didn't
you get the partner you chose?" As people comment, it soon
becomes clear that this has been an exercise in rejection. We
all wanted someone who did not necessarily want us as their
first choice. We have rejected, and we have been rejected. This,
of course, ties into the fear of taking risks.

After more experiences involving vulnerability, we embark on a personal vision exercise. In a meditative setting, we
are encouraged to look closely at our personal values, our talents, our life goals, and obstacles to our life goals. At various
steps in the process, we share these with others and reflect on
them further. We develop a picture of where we would like to
be in the next several years.

Normally, I might have discounted such exercises as fun
but largely crystal gazing. In this case, however, there was something more. I tie its usefulness in my case to my stage in life.
Being at the beginning of midlife, I wanted to examine my life
and my goals for the future. In this sense, I brought to the exercise a readiness to reflect. As well, I am a reflective individual by nature. That the individual participant must have some
inner motivation in this regard is confirmed by research. The
Pecos River program is constantly preparing individuals for self-
examination. Both the silliness exercises and the outdoor adventures are designed to warm up the individual for potentially

profound self-examination. Indeed, for a vision exercise to work, individuals must be warmed up beforehand, I would argue. They must first experience exercises that force self-examination and that encourage questioning of one's goals and purpose. The Pecos River program does a reasonably good job of this.

The exercise began by examining an individual's top talents and values. It did not begin by asking people to explain their vision. It started where it should: by asking what you have valued, enjoyed, and been good at in the past. The assumption is that past successes and talents are what one will build on in the future. The exercise also had individuals visualize their situation one year from that date—not ten years. We know from research that visualization is a potentially powerful tool. In my case, most of what I visualized came true, though some of it took two years to occur. So, the success of the exercise also depends on an individual's ability to be in touch with his or her desires and talents and yet to temper these with realism in imaging the future.

The last morning arrives, and we celebrate and reflect on our experiences. At the close, we are each presented with a small gift—a clip of the kind used by mountain climbers to hook ropes between climbing partners and to scale mountain faces. For us, they will be reminders of risk taking and teamwork.

ARC's VisionQuest

In contrast to the Pecos River program's broad-based approach to issues facing managers, ARC's VisionQuest program focuses on more specific issues, such as the individual's vision (or organizational vision, for company groups). (I would add that I joined the program for individuals, which is more personally oriented than their in-company programs which, I am told, focus on the organization's vision for itself.) The objectives, the contents, of the program are listed in Exhibit 4.1. The emphasis on personal growth is clear in such items as "purpose for living and working" and "being responsible for yourself." Unlike the Pecos River program, however, there are no outdoor-adventure activities. Program content is learned through experiential exer-

Exhibit 4.1. ARC's VisionQuest Topic Areas.

Leadership for organizational results
- Elements of personal effectiveness
- Personal presence

Purpose for living and working
- Discovering your purpose
- Your purpose and your organization's purpose
- Levels of purpose
- Creating consensus and clarity about organizational purpose

Personal and organizational vision
- Identifying and communicating your vision
- Creating common organizational vision
- Action aligned with purpose and vision
- Being responsible for yourself and your results
- Creative risk taking
- The power of commitment

Establishing and maintaining the corporate climate

Creating results
- Putting your vision to work

Source: Copyright ARC International. Reprinted with permission.

cises conducted indoors. Another difference is that participant numbers are smaller and interaction therefore tends to be more intimate in VisionQuest's program. The course content is tailored much more toward personal growth than in the Pecos River program, so the trainer's role as an emotional facilitator becomes more critically important.

The first day of the VisionQuest program, like the first day at the Pecos River Learning Center, is a warming-up experience. There are fourteen of us, mostly middle managers, profit and nonprofit, secluded away in a beautiful lodge in the mountains outside Vail, Colorado. Again, the setting is spectacular and helps to put us all in a positive mind-set. From both the Pecos River program and the VisionQuest experiences, I believe that setting plays a significant role in warming up the mind and emotions to a training experience.

Our trainer, who I will call Jack, shows that he understands the complex issues facing leaders in organizations today.
He is very much a product of the New Age—a thin, athletic
vegetarian in his forties who with his reflective comments prods
and pushes us into thinking about ourselves. Our talks outside
the seminar room are wonderfully personal. As with the setting, the trainer has a definite influence. It is interesting to note
that Jack's presentation is different from the high-energy, enthusiastic facilitators in the Pecos River program. Perhaps this
is because Robert White, the founder of ARC, is less outgoing
and lower key than Larry Wilson. (Might it be that founders
of these programs select trainers, to some extent, in their own
images?)

We begin the program with an engaging video montage
of human faces (most of them smiling, lots of kids), with a theme
song called "It's in Every One of Us." This is clearly meant to
touch our hearts and begin to open us to the possibility of intimacy with our fellow participants.

Throughout the day, Jack employs numerous stories to
convey some of the course's essential values. For instance, he
tells us about a woman friend from Saudi Arabia who is edu-
cated in the United States, where she finds greater opportunities for developing her career and personal life than she would
at home. Going against the demands of her family and her culture, she resists returning to Saudi Arabia, where she would
have to give up her newfound sense of herself. She goes on to
become very successful in the United States. The story teaches
the quandaries that can accompany our efforts to fulfill our own
sense of purpose—the hardships and the trade-offs between personal and career life rewards. It naturally follows that Jack men-
tions that in our preprogram questionnaires the majority of us
have mentioned being out of balance in terms of our personal
and work life.

In ensuing discussion, the aims of VisionQuest are laid
out for us: to give us a deeper sense of who we are, to help us
understand the deep structure of human beings, and to provide
us with models that will help us understand and design our work
in more fulfilling ways. Jack explains how human beings seek

meaning in their work, life, and sense of community, as well as the needs for increasing complexity in work as we achieve objectives. He will build upon these ideas throughout the course.

After presenting his perspective on human nature, Jack talks about the purpose of the training itself: "The real purpose is to create a breakthrough. We want to produce a profound shift in a person. It is our experience that you cannot create a breakthrough in business without first creating a breakthrough for ourselves. [This is a fundamental assumption of these programs.] An effective transformation will reconfigure our whole past so that we experience the world differently and better." The breakthrough, as we will later discover, will come about through a series of intensive exercises involving public declarations of learning from our inquiry into issues that are complex and emotionally demanding.

Jack then asks us, "What is your purpose for being in VisionQuest?" Shortly thereafter, he asks one of us to come to the front of the room to answer the question, "What is the most important thing for you in coming to VisionQuest?" This is the first of numerous public expressions by participants. Jack will use this technique over and over again, seemingly for two purposes: "going public" with one's aims fosters the potential for greater personal commitment (as is indicated by research in psychology), and the need to formulate a coherent statement forces participants to think through and clarify what it is they really want.

Later that afternoon, we are all asked individually to come to the front of the room and tell what our purpose for VisionQuest is. We are also asked to rank, on a scale of 1 through 10 (with 10 the greatest desire), our answer to the question, "How much do you care about getting a personal breakthrough in the program?" The need to make this statement publicly forces participants to think about what they want from the experience, much more so than if no public announcement were to be made.

After each person shares, Jack then asks for their ranking. I say "nine." Many of the participants say "ten," to my surprise. This public ranking serves several purposes. It gives the trainer an immediate sense of who among the participants is committed to the experience and determined, and who will likely resist. It allows Jack to promote one of the important values of the program: "A real problem for many of us is that under conditions of uncertainty and ambiguity we don't want to commit. We just prefer to stay safe. Yet the times are always riddled with uncertainty. People are afraid of committing, even to a sure bet." A "10" is, of course, commitment in this exercise. The exercise then drives home the values of being "fully committed" and of "taking risks." It also psychologically ensures that participants will commit themselves to taking the exercises seriously. This is all part of the warming-up process — building commitment to the unknown that lies ahead.

We move on to the idea of vision. Jack describes visions as arising out of the "nonreasonable part of us": "Vision is in an unreasonable, idealistic part of us. It's a more visceral, emotional quality than logical. It's more, in some sense, an unconscious process. The critical point, however, is to know what you want. Yet very few of us know. A lot of forces on the outside pull us this way and that. So how can we know?" He illustrates the misfortune that can befall a person with an unclear sense of purpose by again telling a story, this time about an African who loses a beautiful spirit wife by being unclear as to what he really wanted from life.

Jack follows his discussion of vision with an exploration of two related issues: entropy and leadership. He describes how organizations, like the human body, break down and must be rebuilt and challenged to stay competitive and how, likewise, visions must constantly be reworked to keep abreast with a changing environment. He moves on to leaders and explains that their roles include managing understanding and creating new organizational contexts or common ground for their followers, as well as helping their organizations avoid entropy. This potpourri of ideas and values, much like the Pecos River program, provides an innovative reflection on the state of business affairs today and presents ideas about organizational change and effectiveness.

Earlier in the day, we were given juggling balls, and we experimented with them, tossing them back and forth with partners. In the evening session and later in the course, these balls will serve as a symbol to illustrate the operating characteristics of organizations. For example, that first day, Jack introduced a model of organizational effectiveness that outlined the critical elements in this order: (1) a resourceful state (the availability of resources such as talent, energy, ideas, funding), (2) a relationship (building trust with partners or co-workers), (3) rapport (communication that works throughout the organization), (4) rhythm (a natural work flow), and (5) the result (the outcome of these steps). An exercise in which we used the juggling balls with partners illustrated this process. After having developed an initial talent of juggling (resourceful state), we had to work closely with our partner (the relationship) and communicate (rapport) how we wished our juggling pattern (rhythm) to go; then our juggling would be successful (result). We also discovered a law of effectiveness: that once we had achieved a rhythm, the game began to lose its appeal, and so we had to create new challenges or rhythms (variety, to ensure challenge) for ourselves.

In retrospect, then, the first day's purpose has been to lay out the idea that vision sets a common understanding and direction for the organization and that leaders create the kind of visions that align with an individual's own personal purposes, visions, and values; that is, that resonate emotionally and psychologically. It is emphasized that, unfortunately, most organizations ask only for action and results, without a common focus or direction, especially one that is meaningful.

The next two days are spent in personal exploration. Again, much of this is warming up for the final days' work on our vision of ourselves. The warm-up now consists of exercises in feedback, personal disclosure, and interpersonal learning experiences. One of the initial exercises is feedback from fellow participants on their perceptions of us. In groups of seven, we take turns receiving feedback on ourselves from the other six members. During the process, the receiver can ask only clarifying questions. Before we begin, a mock run is done between the trainers who model thoughtful, intuitive perceptions. This exercise is to prepare us for further personal disclosure. To my surprise, the exercise works well, in large part, because of the effectiveness and modeling of the trainers. I found the feedback that I received from my group members to be perceptive and accurate, reminding me that many times we have good intuitive perceptions of others, yet we simply do not share them.

A second and personally powerful exercise is called the lifeboat exercise,[3] which goes like this: Fourteen of us are on a sailing boat, and it is sinking. A small life raft is available, but it can hold only three people. We must choose three members of our group whom we feel are worthy of saving. Each of us will have an opportunity to deliver a two-minute "salvation speech" on why we personally should be saved, but we will have only five minutes to prepare it. When everyone has spoken, we will choose the three to be saved, based on their appeals.

I struggle to think of something, not taking the exercise so seriously. In the end, I say something like this: "I thought about the qualities I would look for in someone whom I would save in this exercise, and I decided on three. They are a sense of heart, the possibility of making a contribution to society, and the quality of a good human being. I feel I possess those qualities. I also feel that there are others with those same qualities in the group, and I am willing to sacrifice myself for those individuals." In my clever mind, I have calculated that perhaps the last statement would show a sense of special concern for others and therefore garner me salvation. My cleverness proves to be quite shallow. In the end, I receive only one vote for salvation. Those whom we voted to "save" are the individuals who have truly spoken from their hearts about what remained for them to do in their lives. Several speeches were so emotionally touching that many of us had tears in our eyes. For instance, one woman spoke about her need to heal her relationship with an alcoholic son, whom she loved deeply. Others spoke about deeply personal dreams they had yet to fulfill. This is a powerful exercise, but it requires that enough trust be established in the group to permit self-disclosure.

After each vote, we receive feedback about the impact of our presentation. I will learn that I have come across as too academic and rehearsed, not very much in touch with my emotions, and reluctant to be truly honest with myself about what I wanted. This information was truthful, yet somewhat of a shock. It brought home to me that my public person is at some distance from my personal one. On reflection, I realized that I really would have preferred to have said "I have a lot of unfinished business in my life. I would love to get married and have children. I have my students, whom I love and with whom I still have lots of work to do. I also have many ideas about leadership and training that are unfinished. These are all things of great importance to me, and I would like to have the opportunity to conclude them." It jolted me into thinking about what I really wanted for my future, what really was my unfinished business in life.

While I and several others had a particularly powerful reaction, some participants did not have the same profound reaction. What is important to realize is that this type of exercise has a "hit or miss" quality, depending on the state of mind of each individual participant at the time.

(My understanding is that the lifeboat exercise is no longer done in this form. Specifically because of the reasons I have stated, the new version currently being used is called the acquisition exercise. The trainer starts by describing a scenario in which all of the participants' companies have been acquired in a leveraged takeover. The new emerging company is interested in keeping only three of the strongest leaders. Each participant has the opportunity to declare why he or she should be selected as part of the new management team, based on their skills, abilities, and leadership qualities. The structure of the exercise is similar to the lifeboat exercise. The differences are in the context of the presentations and the feedback to the individuals. In formulating their feedback, the participants are asked to consider their experience of the presenter as a leader, both personally and organizationally. The results of this exercise are described as being as powerful as the lifeboat exercise, but the participants find it significantly more applicable to their professional life.)

By this time, I am thinking about what my emotions want, and why am I out of touch with them. As well, I ask myself why I have to provide a public image that is separated from my internal self. In essence, what ARC is arguing is that alignment must occur between our purpose/vision, our emotions, and the domain in which we wish to work. The key ideas of the course become (1) aligning with our real self (lifeboat exercise), (2) getting in touch with our vision and values (visioning and legacy exercises), (3) putting this into action (the juggling exercises and action plans for our lives), and (4) encouraging vulnerability in doing all of this (the personal disclosure exercises).

As we work through the exercises, we participants are bombarded with feedback about our lives. I am continually reminded of my personal gifts, such as my ability to be articulate, my intellect, and so on. So, on the one hand, there is empowerment and confidence building. On the other hand, I am powerfully reminded of my weaknesses, such as processing life through my head rather than my heart, being self-oriented, and so on. In this respect, the ARC program is more reflective than the Pecos River program and forces participants to probe more deeply into themselves. This is a function of ARC's strong orientation to personal growth, the small size of the group, and the trainer's skill and experience.

Interspersed throughout these several days we find ourselves in more juggling exercises, in which we attempt to make elegant and creative organizations of jugglers, and in trust exercises. We hear short lectures on how human beings seek and need challenge, on "flow" theory (special states when people are functioning most effectively and most creatively), and so on. The result is mixed in terms of our ability to integrate all of this while we are digesting our more emotional experiences. As with the Pecos River program, very few participants will remember any of the models or theories. It is the personal experiences that will have a more lasting impact. (I understand from ARC, however, that their own substantial research on VisionQuest graduates indicates strong recall of specific leadership models.)

From my own perspective, the program's real strength is in providing participants with an opportunity to get in touch with a highly personal vision. It is less effective on models, on links back to organizational life, on skills and techniques. I find that when a variety of models and theories are presented, participants have a relatively difficult time integrating them into the training experience. For this reason, programs built around a single model (such as The Leadership Challenge) are more effective in terms of participants' recall and later utilization of a model.

There are, however, some successful attempts to integrate concepts into experiences. At one point, we are discussing the idea of flow. We are told that flow states have a pattern, repeat that pattern, and yet are also complex and challenging. We integrate these ideas into a juggling exercise wherein we must figure out a juggling pattern among all of us that is creative and simple, yet sufficiently complex to be challenging, and that has a symmetry and pattern! We eventually create it, but it is short-lived, as boredom with the game soon settles in. We then have to change our pattern to maintain our interest in the activity.

One of the difficulties that all training programs face is how to find effective metaphors for the work organization. For the Pecos River program, the cliff jump is a metaphor for risk taking in life. In the ARC program, the juggling balls become "our job," and "our organization" is our group juggling. We attempt to integrate workplace ideas through the metaphorical experience of the juggling game. It is difficult to say whether these experiences really are effective metaphors, but this is the constant challenge of training: how to simulate organizational realities outside of the organization.

Although juggling is still used as a metaphor in the VisionQuest program, I understand that many opportunities to address issues that are specific to each participant's business environment have been designed into the program. New additions also include models regarding responsibility, partnership, levels of agreement, and commitment among others, all of which apply directly to participants' organizations. One specific model is called the Eight Elements of Personal and Organizational Effectiveness (see Exhibit 4.2). This includes an inquiry into our relationship to these eight characteristics, which ARC has found consistently in effective leaders.

Exhibit 4.2. ARC's Eight Elements of
Personal and Organizational Effectiveness.

---

1. Decide . . . clearly, specifically and postively what you want.
2. Be Honest . . . to yourself and others.
3. Express Yourself . . . acknowledge your unique contribution and make it.
4. Take Risks . . . that are appropriate and responsible.
5. Participate 100 Percent . . . in everything you do.
6. Be Responsible . . . take ownership for your choices.
7. Create Partnership . . . participate with others in a mutually beneficial manner.
8. Commit . . . be willing to commit 100 percent, doing what it takes.

Source: Copyright ARC International. Reprinted with permission.

The final days of the program are spent finalizing personal visions and what are called our "personal statements." We
begin with a "lifeline exercise," which examines our life at birth
and stretches through the past to the present and on to the future. Jack instructs us as follows: "I want you to go back in the
time line, but be above it and watch. Go back as early as you
can, looking for patterns and themes. The last frame will be
the present. Then we'll zip all the way out to the end of your
life in terms of where you might be and the people who will
be around you. Don't create a disaster ending, but a good ending. You have two criteria at the end: (1) you are in a state of
completion, and (2) you are in a state of gratitude. It is the perfect ending. That means there is a certain way you have lived
to have reached that end state. Then look back and see how
you lived that brought you to that state. How would you have
lived that would create that state of completion and gratitude?"

The idea of this exercise is to "envision" an ideal future
for ourselves. By doing so, we quickly get in touch with those
aspects of our lives that we most value. What emerges for most
of us is the importance of family and personal relationships. Our
careers play a role, but with the time line going out to old age,
their significance diminishes somewhat. This exercise essentially
allows us to consciously brainstorm out what we most desire
in life to feel "completed." This is just one in a series of exercises that push us to come to grips with the discrepancies between who we are and who we wish to become.

This is one of the last preparations before our "personal stand" exercise, which occurs on the next-to-last day of the seminar. Jack instructs us: "You are going to come up with a stand that is at the center of you — the 'me.' It will be your most resourceful state. The first rule is that you cannot tell someone else what their stand should be. I want you to come back tomorrow with a set of words that are your own stand. Rule number two: no negative words. Instead it needs to be a word that takes you toward something. Rule number three: this is not a paragraph, just a few words. It has a single poetry to it. Nothing tentative about it. The stand is essentially a personal mantra for you. Everyone will come to the front of the room and give their stand. The audience will vote on how the statement affects them. We will be a tuning fork. When someone states their stand, and you as an audience member feel that it is just right for that person, then stand up and show your support." Each of us must then choose a phrase that captures where we want to be, and it must be heartful and truthful enough to convince our audience that it really represents our inner desires. By this point in the seminar, our fellow participants have become very effective at gauging our sincerity. We know that we will be a tough audience for one another.

I struggle that evening over what my stand is to be. It has become very clear to me that I want to be more personally expressive of my opinions and emotional reactions. The week has forced me to reflect on the fact that my public persona — my need to be seen as a diplomatic and sensitive individual — gets in the way, at times, of my asserting my own opinion or getting into conflicts over an issue. After some contemplation, I decide that my stand must reflect more risk taking. The Pecos River program (which I participated in before ARC) has also been a catalyst for risk taking, and my experiences there reinforce a decision to have a risk orientation in my stand. The risk, of course, is in being more open about my concerns and emotions. "I am a risk-oriented individual" doesn't quite capture my feelings, so after several iterations I decide on using the word "courage." I later learn from a fellow participant that it is derived from a word meaning "heart." Knowing this, the term seems even more appropriate, given my experience in the lifeboat exercise, when I failed to speak from my heart. Finally, I settle on the statement "I am a courageous man."

For the average person outside the context of the Vision-Quest seminar, this might seem like navel-gazing. Yet, it is a relatively successful exercise. It follows an important law of training, which we have learned from our research with participants: focus on a few simple ideas. Moreover, the statement looks simple, but it is in fact the product of a week's worth of soul-searching. Also, everyone's stand appears to represent a certain fortitude or a positive emotional state they need to be in *now* in order to face important issues in their careers or personal life. Finally, each person's stand must pass the test of sincerity, as judged by peers.

Our fellow participants, as it turns out, are indeed quite tough. Less than a majority of us make it through the first round of public statements. Each individual goes to the front and states his or her stand. So, for example, someone might say, "I am a lovable person." Jack will take lots of time to clarify with that individual each word of the statement. He or she must explain on a personal, feeling level what "lovable" means. It is a very demanding process. Some of us rise up immediately (the means of voting) for an individual's stand. The "holdouts," however, force individuals to deepen their stands in terms of their emotional commitment. One individual says, "I am an honest man who will make a difference." Jack has him change it to the present tense — "who is making a difference" — so that the individual feels he is currently in that emotional space. There are many subtleties to this interaction among the presenter, Jack, and peers that cannot be captured.

After most of us have had our stands accepted, we go back to juggling exercises. Later we will return to those who must rework their stands. This time, the juggling will be a finale, wherein we have to create a process among all group members that is beautiful, symmetrical, generative, creative, stable, and fun. We are given two hours to create a pattern that meets all these criteria. In some surprising ways, this exercise mimics organizational reality. I watch as leaders rise and fall in the game. Apathy appears. Some of us take responsibility; others back off.

There are moments of chaos as one group of us wants to do one thing while another wants to do another—just as organizational departments fight for their outcomes. The exercise again illustrates how organizational realities evolve. Its weakness is that its lessons are difficult to learn or to transfer back to the workplace because the ideas of rhythm and flow are not well connected to our own organizational situations. In addition, many of these concepts are difficult to ground in "how to's."

The last day is spent finalizing personal visions for our future. Our visions are statements that focus on our purpose in life and are slightly more complicated than the personal stand. They generally reflect our desires to be more integrated individuals. Again, the focus is more on the personal side than the career side. So, for example, one participant describes her resolution to form a pact with her husband that every night before going to bed they will address their unresolved issues of the day. In general, statements are quite personal and moving. As is now the norm, we present our visions publicly. Finally, Jack closes the session by reaffirming the importance of leadership and by commenting on how much more accurately we know ourselves than when we began the program.

ARC continually evaluates its programs and has made a number of design changes since I participated in the Vision-Quest program. I understand that many of the changes are reflected in some of the feedback I offered about the program. The current model has a greater focus on specific, real organizational issues. Although participants continue to regard VisionQuest as a significant personal experience, the purpose of the conversations and processes throughout the program now, I am told, speak directly to developing leadership in organizations and in life.

Chapter Five

Understanding the Leadership Difference: The Conceptual Approaches

A scholar once asked Alfred North Whitehead, the British mathematician and philosopher, which he believed to be more important, ideas or things. "Why, I should imagine ideas **about** things," Whitehead replied.

— Clifton Fadiman

Next to the skill-building approaches to leadership training, conceptual training has been the most popular. Educators assume that we can best understand a complex subject — including leadership — if we start with a conceptual overview of it. With the big picture in mind, we set about learning the particulars — how to become a leader, in this case. As well, formulating a concept of our subject allows us to frame its character concretely, so that we are able to distinguish it mentally from other constructs that may or may not be related — in our case, we distinguish leadership behavior from managership behavior. Presumably, with this distinction in mind, a manager can set about practicing the behaviors of a leader and become one.[1]

A program highly representative of the conceptual approach is The Leadership Challenge™, developed by James M. Kouzes and Barry Z. Posner.[2] Most programs that teach applied

84

leadership training employ a certain model of leadership (for example, the Forum) or a range of models (for example, the Pecos River program), but few are built so tightly around one particular conceptual understanding of the art as is The Leadership Challenge. Using a five-step model of leadership, the course maps out for participants the behaviors associated with each of the steps. These are illustrated through lectures, films, and discussions. Skill-building exercises, outdoor-adventure activities, and feedback further ground the concept in leadership actions.

The Program Designers and Their Aims

The program is the result of research that Jim Kouzes and Barry Posner formulated into a book entitled *The Leadership Challenge: How to Get Extraordinary Things Done in Organizations* (Jossey-Bass, 1987). Seminars based on the book's findings are offered both for the public at large and for organizational groups. Public programs are normally taught by Jim Kouzes and Barry Posner, while in-company and other programs are taught by members of the Tom Peters Group/Learning Systems staff, contract trainers, or in-company trainers. The model developed in the book and promoted in the seminars is based on a research project begun in 1983. Jim and Barry investigated what leaders did when they performed at their "personal best" in leading, not managing, others. Their "personal best" survey consisted of thirty-eight open-ended questions and included questions such as, Who initiated the project? What special techniques or strategies did you use to get other people involved in the project? What did you learn about leadership from this project? The survey required up to two hours to complete, and ultimately some 550 surveys were collected. The authors also report their ongoing collection of case studies, now in the thousands. A shorter, two-page survey was completed by an additional 780 managers. As well, 42 individuals were interviewed in depth. The participants were all middle-level and senior-level managers in private- and public-sector organizations. From this study, five general practices and ten behavioral commitments were identified. These are listed in Exhibit 5.1. The Leadership Practices Inventory

Exhibit 5.1. Practices of Exemplary Leaders.

Challenging the Process
- Searching for Opportunities
- Experimenting

Inspiring a Shared Vision
- Envisioning the Future
- Enlisting Others

Enabling Others to Act
- Strengthening Others
- Fostering Collaboration

Modeling the Way
- Setting an Example
- Planning Small Wins

Encouraging the Heart
- Celebrating Accomplishments
- Recognizing Contributions

---

was developed from this research, and it is used as a principal feedback source in the course. The inventory is the result of extensive research, and today over 35,000 inventory respondents are included in the database. (Several doctoral dissertations have been written using the Leadership Practices Inventory as part of the research, and all report similarly strong validity and reliability.)

The designers, Jim and Barry, at one time worked together at the Leavey School of Business and Administration at Santa Clara University in California. Barry, a past director of the school's MBA program, is currently a professor of management. His interest in leadership is a result of participation in campus political activity during the 1960s and a one-time desire to become a Supreme Court justice. Jim, who is currently the president of TPG/Learning Systems (A Tom Peters Group Company), was the director of the Executive Development Center at the Leavey School of Business and Administration, and was a member of the Peace Corps during the 1960s. Both men have had extensive experience training line managers from private and public corporations. The Leadership Challenge is a natural by-product of their backgrounds as both students and practitioners of leadership.

The Leadership Challenge Program

When I first sit down to a table to find a binder, pads of paper, and all the other paraphernalia of the seminar, I am struck by the cover of my Leadership Challenge binder. On it is a large stylized image of a compass, which soon proves to be a symbol for the course. Not surprisingly, after instructor and participant introductions, our first activity involves an orienteering exercise. We are asked to form groups of five. We are then given compasses and instructions, and each group is asked to find different green owls hidden outside. So we begin the course by acting out its theme: the idea of a team developing its sense of direction.

After this initial symbolic exercise, Jim Kouzes opens the evening by outlining our objectives for the next several days (see Exhibit 5.2). He then reviews what we had submitted as our objectives or hoped-for outcomes from the seminar and indicates how these will be addressed. This initial evening is essentially an introduction to the course and its ideas, and includes our first exercise, which is in skill building. We are told there is a table at the back of the seminar room that is covered with toys and gimmicks — our "awards" table. We are asked to practice the "encouraging" dimension of their model by spontaneously handing out these toys to fellow participants whom we feel have contributed to us in some way. According to participants, this proved to be a highly effective skill-building exercise. After returning to their work, many actively rewarded others at the office.

As "pre-work," we have completed the Personal Best Questionnaire. The Personal Best Questionnaire is designed to elicit information about our individual standards of excellence through our written descriptions of one leadership experience that each

Exhibit 5.2. The Program Schedule
of The Leadership Challenge Workshop™.

TPG/Learning Systems
A Tom Peters Group Company
Workshop Design

Tuesday
3:30 P.M.   Arrival
             - Pick up name tags and agenda
             - Check into rooms
4:00 P.M.   Orientation to the Journey
             - The route we're going to travel
             - Expectations of what the journey will be like
             - The members of the team
5:30 P.M.   Refreshments
6:15 P.M.   Dinner
7:30 P.M.   Our Leadership Bests
             - Our Personal Best Cases
             - Leadership lessons from experience
10:00 P.M.   Adjourn

Wednesday
7:00 A.M.   Breakfast
8:00 A.M.   The Practices of Exemplary Leadership
             - The Kouzes-Posner leadership model
             - The Leadership Practices Inventory
10:15 A.M.   Break
10:30 A.M.   Challenging the Process
             - Conditions that foster leadership
             - Outsight and insight
             - The hardiness factor
11:15 A.M.   Challenges in Our Own Lives
             - The peaks and valleys of experience
             - Themes and patterns from our past
             - Briefing on the "Ropes Course"
12:00 P.M.   Lunch
1:00 P.M.   Experience Challenge
             - The Ropes Course: A series of outdoor initiatives
3:00 P.M.   Break
3:30 P.M.   Learning from Experience
             - Personal lessons from the Ropes Course
             - Relating the lessons to leadership
4:30 P.M.   Inspiring a Shared Vision
             - One leader's image of the future
             - The meaning of vision
             - Giving life to a vision

Exhibit 5.2. The Program Schedule
of The Leadership Challenge Workshop™, Cont'd.

5:30 P.M.   Clarifying Your Own Vision
            - What is your ideal and unique image of the future?
            - Getting others to see what you see
7:30 P.M.   Dinner
9:00 P.M.   Optional Activities
            - Video of the Ropes Course
            - Reading
            - Talking with friends

Thursday
7:00 A.M.   Breakfast
8:00 A.M.   Experiencing Teamwork and Trust
            - Why you have to give to get
            - The Ropes Course: more outdoor initiatives
10:10 A.M. Break
10:45 A.M. Learning from Experience
            - Personal learnings from the Ropes Course
            - Relating the learnings to leadership
11:30 A.M. Enabling Others to Act (I)
            - Developing cooperative goals and building trust
            - How to expand other people's influence
12:15 P.M. Lunch
1:15 P.M.   Enabling Others to Act (II)
            - How one leader strengthens others
            - How to empower others
2:30 P.M.   Break
2:50 P.M.   What Followers Expect of Their Leaders
            - The other half of the leadership study
            - Leadership and credibility
3:15 P.M.   Developing Our Own Leadership Credo
            - How shared values make a difference
            - Writing our guiding principles
3:45 P.M.   Break
4:00 P.M.   Modeling the Way
            - How one leader sets the example
            - How to be a role model for others
            - How to build commitment
5:00 P.M.   Break
5:15 P.M.   Encouraging the Heart
            - How one leader celebrates and recognizes others
            - How to link rewards and performance
            - Maintaining high expectations
6:15 P.M.   Making Commitments
            - Personal planning
            - Making commitments for the next twenty-one days

Exhibit 5.2. The Program Schedule
of The Leadership Challenge Workshop™, Cont'd.

	- Swapping techniques
	- Tomorrow's agenda
7:30 P.M.	Dinner
9:00 P.M.	Optional Activities
	- Video of Ropes Course
	- Meeting with friends
	- Reading
	- Conversation
Friday	
7:00 A.M.	Breakfast
8:00 A.M.	Presentation Planning
	- Reviewing visions, values, and actions
	- Writing a five minute "stump speech"
	- Group assignments
9:15 A.M.	Presentations
	- Giving your "stump speech"
	- Getting constructive feedback from colleagues
11:30 A.M.	Celebration Planning
	- Group planning for recognizing others
	- Check out of rooms
12:15 P.M.	Celebrating Our Accomplishments
	- Group awards and recognition
	- Presentation of certificates
	- Toasts and farewells
1:15 P.M.	The Last Lunch
2:00 P.M.	Bon Voyage

of us believes illustrates a peak personal performance. The personal bests exercise calls for each participant to look at his or her own leadership "best" in the group and to search for patterns. Exhibit 5.3 explains the nature of a "personal best."

While originally scheduled for the first evening, our personal leadership best case discussions begin the next morning. In teams of five, we are asked to identify the practices of leadership common to all our experiences. So that we are not influenced by the designer's conclusions, The Leadership Challenge model is not yet introduced. The participant groups in essence

Exhibit 5.3. Getting Started.

Personal Best. A "personal best" experience is an event (or series of events) that you believe to be your individual standard of excellence. It is your own "record-setting performance," a time when you did your very best. It is something you use to measure yourself by, a time you look upon as your peak performance experience. A useful and simple guide to the selection of your "personal best" is "When I think about this, it makes me smile a lot."

Leadership Experience. You have been involved in many experiences in your career. For purposes of this exercise, we ask that you focus your thinking on only those in which you were the leader. You might use these criteria to select your leadership experience:

1. Your experience does not need to be restricted to a time when you were an appointed or selected leader. It can be either a time when you emerged as the informal leader or a time when you were the official leader or manager.

2. It can be in any functional area, in a service or manufacturing organization, in a public or private institution, in a staff or line position.

3. It can be the start-up of a new business, a new product or service development program, a quality or productivity improvement project, and so on.

4. The experience does not need to have occurred in your present organization; it could be a past work experience. It could also have occurred in a club, a professional organization, a school, or any other setting. Let it be any time when you felt that you performed at your very best as a leader.

---

become researchers and attempt to develop their own theory by examining their own and others' personal best stories. The teams disperse for brainstorming, and then return to the conference room to present findings. Our group, for example, presents five themes of our leadership personal bests: the situation involved (1) a tough challenge, (2) a vision, (3) a team, (4) leadership by example, and (5) fun and celebration. Other teams mentioned vision, challenge, risk taking, recognition, commitment, communication, a high degree of freedom, trust, a long time frame, teamwork, and challenging the status quo. In the end, the individual group findings prove to be remarkably close to and consistent with the model that will soon be presented.

The Personal Best exercise helps us to reflect on our own experience and then to compare our experiences with the seminar's conclusions, which ultimately gives great credibility to what is about to be presented. This is a particularly powerful exercise and is unique to The Leadership Challenge program. Many of us begin to see more clearly the ingredients of our own leadership experiences, that is, specifically what we did to lead successfully. Those of us who are not feeling like leaders are reminded that we have the capacity to be leaders nonetheless. In my case, I am reminded that I have the capacity to be a strong leader and yet am not acting on it, a reminder that rekindles the desire to one day lead my own organization.

This exercise helps us to realize that leadership ability is lying dormant in many of us. The positioning of the exercise at the beginning of the course opens participants to realizing that leadership is not an elusive quality accessible to only a few. As a result, the desire to learn and experiment with the practices we are about to learn is heightened, and we discuss some of the subtler aspects of leadership. For example, some idealized aspects of leadership are mentioned. In my group, a few members assert that leaders have balance in their lives. I note that, quite to the contrary, their lives are often unbalanced. Discussion continues, but we reach no conclusions on the issue.

Barry Posner then gets us to summarize the general observations we can make about leadership based on our personal bests experience. He points out that because we have all had some positive leadership experience we therefore all have the potential to be leaders again. Once again, the idea is to point out that leadership is not a mystical force that one is born with or not; rather, that it is a skill that can be developed by coaching and through experience.

Jim Kouzes takes over to discuss why leadership is more critical today than ever, given the turbulent economy, intense competitive pressures, rapidly changing technologies, and market demands for quality. His conclusion: today's instability demands more leaders. He sets the stage for explaining why so many more organizations are in need of leadership today than in the past. He then distinguishes between the leadership skills of yesterday and today, arguing that today's leaders must be more inspirational and collaborative. This discussion leads quite naturally to the five practices of The Leadership Challenge model:

1. Challenging the Process
2. Inspiring a Shared Vision
3. Enabling Others to Act
4. Modeling the Way
5. Encouraging the Heart

Using slides, with quotations and pictures, Jim will tell many stories, often humorous and inspirational, to illustrate the five key leadership practices of their framework. References to our personal best leadership experiences will be woven into the presentation. For example, at one point, he puts up a slide of a statement: "Anything worth doing is worth doing poorly." Like a zen koan, the motto takes the viewer aback for a moment because, on the surface, it seems an outrageous statement. After a moment's puzzling, participants realize the true message: in undertaking anything of importance, we will always encounter failure or mistakes; we must learn from these and continue to press on. Jim asks: "Think back to the first day you learned a new sport. Did you do it perfectly? Or the time you first used a personal computer. What happened the first day, in terms of improving your productivity? It got worse, didn't it?" He is preparing us to accept the idea that risk and the possibility of failure are parts of any worthwhile undertaking; they are also essential parts of leadership. The key idea is that whenever individuals or organizations make major transitions, they get worse before they get better.

This discussion is designed to illustrate the ideas behind the program's first practice: "Challenging the Process." It is an attempt to get participants thinking about their own status quo and how to challenge it — recognizing that any such attempts will meet with resistance, but that one must persevere. This idea is experientially grounded in an outdoor ropes course that afternoon.

Jim and Barry use the morning of the second day to introduce each step of their model, using examples and stories to illustrate their points. Late that morning, Barry goes over the Leadership Practices Inventory (LPI), which they have developed from their model. They explain its validity as an assessment instrument as the principal feedback mechanism in the course. Afterward, we receive feedback from our self-evaluations and evaluations by our subordinates, bosses, and peers who have filled out inventory forms about us. The LPI provides us with others' feedback as well as self-reports on the five leadership practices. Specifically, we receive feedback on six behaviors related to each practice. So, for example, under the practice of "challenging the process," there will be assessments of my ability to "challenge the status quo," "look for innovative opportunities," "experiment and take risks," and so on. We discuss among ourselves what about the results pleased us and what surprised us. I will learn that I am strong on challenging, enabling, and encouraging, and slightly weaker on inspiring and modeling. The instrument then helps us to focus on areas we need to develop and identify parts of the course we will want to pay particular attention to.

The morning closes with a discussion by Jim on the fact that leadership begins with a challenge, not, usually, a clear vision — an important distinction. In an exercise drawing on our personal bests project, we are asked to describe the character and feel of the class "bests" experience. We brainstorm in small groups and then as an entire class. What emerges is a list of terms such as "high energy" and "uplifting." From this, Jim draws the connection that it is the feel of the challenge that is the first step in the leadership process. Vision will come later.

The afternoon begins with a ropes course. As individuals, we ascend trees and jump out to grab ropes or walk across narrow boards suspended high between trees. There are also on-the-ground exercises that we perform in teams. The tree exercises introduce the notions and feelings of challenge, risk taking, and group support, while the ground exercises build teamwork. Though simpler in format than the Pecos River program's exercises, these appear almost as effective in terms of emotional impact, according to participants' comments. Also, like the Pecos River program's exercises, these attempt to show the important links between trust and success. This was a particularly significant part of the course for a number of participants.

On our return from the outdoors, Barry asks us to describe what was most helpful for each of us in the process. We again

brainstorm out a list: "an environment of support," "encouragement," "each step of the process was explained," "we publicly
recognized everyone's accomplishments," "we tested to see if each
of us needed help."

Barry helps us to draw the links between the ropes exercises and organizational life. He points out that many times the
organization is not a trusting environment, that people are asked
to take risks and then the system lets them down, and so on.
It becomes clear that the primary purpose of the exercise is to
show how important a trusting system is—that an organizational
system supportive of risk and constructive failure is crucial if
the people in it are to be effective.

Jim moves the discussion toward the importance of leadership and risk taking with a story of ballerinas. He tells of a
research project that compared artists and managers in which
a social scientist interviewed a teacher of ballet and asked her
about her young ballerinas. "Could you ever tell when a young
girl would become a prima ballerina?" he asks. The teacher
responds that while all the girls were limber and very flexible
when young, the prima ballerinas were the ones who were willing to make fools of themselves. This, Jim argues, is also the
mark of a good leader. He ties the logic back to the ropes exercise by saying that most of us believe we can jump from one
point to another without taking risks (by analogy, we can make
organizational changes without taking risks). In reality, risk is
an essential part of the experience, as we learned in taking the
risk of jumping from a tree on the ropes course. This is a real
"aha" experience for many of us, as the program drives home
the idea of risk taking and leadership.

We then shift to the second practice, "Inspiring a Shared
Vision." Jim begins by demystifying the idea of vision. He uses
the example of Martin Luther King, Jr., stating his vision for
black Americans in powerful terms, and contrasts this with a
hypothetical scenario of King on the steps of the Lincoln Me-
morial in 1963 saying, "I have absolutely no idea where we are
going. Why don't you form a few small groups and talk about it?"

Sandwiched between Jim's points are slides of key statements, such as "Leaders choose to invent the future rather than

wait for someone else." Each slide drives home succinctly the idea Jim is trying to capture in his stories or examples. It is a memorable means of conveying the central ideas. Jim also uses humor, especially in thought-provoking stories, to illustrate his points. For example, to illustrate what the lack of vision can mean to an organization, he describes the following scenario: "My job requires that I fly a lot, so I have become an experienced traveler. I pack only two bags, one to go under my seat, and one to go overhead or in the hanging compartment. I also get my boarding pass and seat assignment ahead of time. Now, imagine that I go to the airport this afternoon to fly to San Francisco. With my two bags, my boarding pass, and my seat assignment, all I have to do is check the monitor and locate the gate to San Francisco. So I do, and guess what? The monitors are blank. Now I have to go stand in line with all the other passengers. I eventually get to the front of the line, but time is passing, and I hurriedly ask the agent for the gate to San Francisco. The agent looks at me apologetically and says, 'I am sorry, sir, but there is no gate assignment to San Francisco. Any gate will do.' I'm puzzled and disgusted, but being a frequent flier and anxious to get home, I look for someone who I think knows what's what. I find a pilot — you know, the one with the stripes on the sleeve and the scrambled eggs on the hat. Really running late now, I say breathlessly, 'Captain, you must know where these planes are going. I've got my two bags, one over and one under, my boarding pass, and my seat assignment. All I need to know is the gate to San Francisco. Can you tell me where it is?' The captain looks perplexed and responds, 'I'm sorry, sir, there is no gate assignment for San Francisco. Any gate will do. We pilots make up our minds once we get in the air.'"

This story illustrates that if leaders are unclear about their direction and destination, their constituents will suffer from discomfort and stress. For leaders to be influential, they must be able to articulate their "vision of the future" in ways that uplift and attract others.

Jim also relates stories about managers and leaders to illustrate the model's key ideas. It is quite helpful that many of these stories tell about midlevel managers who are attempting to change their organizations, rather than about high-level business leaders like Iacocca. Since most of our group are midlevel managers, this approach demystifies the fact that the five practices are not reserved for senior executives.

To encourage thinking about the process of envisioning, Jim uses another analogy to travel. He asks our group what we would do if we were going to visit London for the first time. We quickly brainstorm a list of activities such as getting travel information, talking to people who have already visited London, buying travel books, and talking to a travel agent who is knowledgeable about London. We then apply this principle to visions, the idea being that one must seek out as much information as possible in the area of his or her vision. One must read what futurists have to say, what demographics seem to indicate, what the industry trends seem to be, and so on. Jim argues that the quality of one's vision depends on how much information gathering one has done.

Jim moves to an audio recording of Martin Luther King, Jr., delivering his famous speech on the steps of the Lincoln Monument in Washington, D.C. We listen to King's speech and afterward discuss how he constructed it to inspire his audience. We identify the following key elements: (1) passion in his voice, (2) repetition of key ideas, (3) the moving phrase "I have a dream," (4) themes tied to American ideal of "liberty and justice for all," (5) powerful contrasts in his images, and (6) the positive connections between blacks and whites. The idea of this exercise is to have participants connect vision with a sense of passion and, presumably, higher purpose. King then becomes a model for us of a leader with a true vision.

Rather than teaching "visioning skills" directly, Jim demonstrates our potential to be more visionary by using a guided fantasy exercise. We are told that we are cinematographers and that Robert Redford has come to us asking for help designing an opening scene for a new film. He has already picked out the music. We are to listen to seven minutes of the music and then write down whatever images, feelings, colors, and scenes come to our minds.

As I listen to the music, which is Pachelbel's Canon in D, I imagine a winter scene. I see snow falling, and then my "camera" pans to the inside of a home. It is a wood-paneled living room, with a fire in the fireplace. Six adults and a small child are sitting in the room. They are laughing and playing. A dog appears, chasing a ball thrown by the child. The camera then centers on a woman who is talking and smiling. A man appears at the door. Everyone greets him, and again there are lots of smiles and laughter. I am constructing a film about the relationship between the man and woman. I am surprised at how quickly and creatively I am able to envision such a scenario. It reaffirms my potential to be creative when I need to be.

We use the exercise to connect with our ability to imagine. We discuss how most of us have been able to visualize some rich images, that certain important values play out in our scenarios, and that we have produced a significant amount of detail, given the brevity of the exercise. Jim points out that this exercise demonstrates that we all have the power to communicate an image or idea. This warm-up leads to a personal vision exercise that we do on our own.

Using a seminar notebook containing a series of questions about our personal vision, we reflect on what we want to accomplish in our work. We contemplate such questions as, What do I want to accomplish? Why do I want to do this? How do I want to change the world for myself and my organization? What mission absolutely obsesses me? What is my dream about my work? About what do I have a burning passion? I reflect on my desire to be a great teacher. As well, we are asked to think about the people or groups who we need to enlist in realizing our vision. Then we develop images, metaphors, and symbols for our visions. After an hour of reflection, we return to the conference room, pick a partner, and share our insights. Later that evening we are invited to watch a videotape of our experiences on the ropes course that day. Most of us stay and relive the energy, challenge, and camaraderie.

The next morning we return to the ropes course for more outdoor adventures. Exercises center around teamwork and the development of group trust. For example, in the trust fall, we each fall backward into the arms of our fellow participants. Then, blindfolded, we as a team must create a perfect square using a long piece of rope and communicating only with words. Finally, as an entire group, we are asked to devise a means of lifting a barrel and moving it outside a circle of rope, using ropes, a tire, and other miscellaneous materials. We form four teams, and each team meets to decide what would be the most effective approach. Each team then appoints a leader to represent its opinion to the other groups. The four group leaders meet to negotiate a solution. What occurs is that the leaders chose a solution unrelated to our own team's. I watch as our team members quickly begin to lose interest in the project; we have not had ownership of the solution, and so, as in real organizational life, we become disinterested.

These and other exercises emphasize the necessity of teamwork to succeed. Back in the seminar room, we reflect on what we have learned. This leads to the next step in the Kouzes-Posner model, "Enabling Others to Act." We learn that trust and support are critical in any task, that a willingness to listen to other perspectives and to develop shared goals is important to effectiveness, and that a positive working environment facilitates success.

We also discuss what we have learned in terms of leadership. We reflect on the fact that a leader provides a certain rhythm for the group, that leaders must constantly communicate, and that they must encourage followers to speak and be heard. What follows are videos on effective leaders that demonstrate how they enable subordinates. This leads to a discussion of the process of empowerment. In small groups, we brainstorm the conditions that have led to our feeling powerful and powerless. From this, we identify conditions of power related to (1) having important tasks to do, (2) discretion on the job, (3) visibility for our work, and (4) connections to others. We discuss how these insights might be applied in our organizations.

"Modeling the Way," the fourth practice, focuses on how a leader sets an example for others. We begin by reviewing a list of twenty characteristics of superior leaders as identified in a study of North American and European managers. Individually we rank these characteristics, and then the results are tabulated with those of the rest of the group. "Honest" proves to be the number one characteristic, followed by "Forward Looking," "Inspiring," "Competent," and "Broadminded." A ten-minute video is introduced that shows subordinates describing the importance to them of these characteristics in their managers.

Jim and Barry point out the remarkable similarity between our group's ranking of these important leader qualities and how they are ranked in their overall sample (numbering more than 25,000 respondents). They go on to point out that the top three — honest, competent, and inspiring — are also the qualities that communication resources refer to as "source credibility." Followers most expect credibility from their leaders, and that credibility is based on trustworthiness (honesty), expertise (competence), and dynamism (inspiring). Yet, as Jim argues, the credibility of those in official positions is declining. He cites study results that show that less than 30 percent of subordinates believe their managers know what they are doing. The question then becomes, How do I, as a leader, build credibility?

Citing the research of others, along with their own, Jim tells us that when followers perceive top management to have high credibility, they are more likely to be proud to tell others they are part of the company, talk up the organization with friends, see their own values as similar to the organization's, and feel a sense of ownership for the organization. Leaders must guard their credibility carefully. It is hard to earn, and easy to lose by a careless act or misspoken word.

Referring to the Leadership Practices Inventory, we learn that the two priorities most significantly associated with credibility (from the subordinates' perspective) are the extent to which leaders "inspire a shared vision" and "model the way." In other words, leaders must be forward looking and communicate their vision by behavior that demonstrates competence, enthusiasm, and honesty.

We are asked at this point to apply the credibility issue to our own work situations. Then we are asked what we believe in, what our leadership philosophy is. This exercise is grounded in a memorandum exercise in which we write a memo to our staff back at the office. We are instructed to map out our operating principles and our important values for our staff to use while we are away on a six-month sabbatical. We all begin with the following statement: "I have decided to take a six-month sabbatical. During that time I will be unable to communicate with you in any way—not by letter, telephone, fax, E-mail, or messenger. Therefore, I have written the following memo on how I would like you to run our business in my absence."

I describe the way I wish my students to be treated, and say that a top-ranking professor must take my place, one who is challenging, real-world oriented, entertaining, and caring. I want clients referred only to two special people. I give instructions to make certain my secretary is treated well, and so on. In essence, my statement maps out some of my basic values about my work and the people I work for. This exercise takes ten minutes, and then we share in pairs. Some people find this easy, others find it difficult. We all agree that it should be easy and we gain insight from the experience of trying to distill the essence of our leadership philosophy and what we care about the most in our lives and organizations.

After a break, we return to watch a segment from the film *In Search of Excellence,* about Stew Leonard, a charismatic entrepreneur who owns a very special supermarket. He is shown modeling leadership behavior as he moves through his store; particular emphasis is placed on consumer service. Jim then tells the story of Thomas Watson, Jr., the former chairman of IBM, who while touring an area of IBM was stopped by a security guard. The guard informed Watson that he needed a security badge to enter a restricted area. Watson looked at the guard and said, "He's right." A badge was obtained for him before he entered the restricted area.

This story is contrasted with another true incident of a CEO who stopped in to look at the engagement book at the receptionist's desk. As he lifted it off her desk, she grabbed it back saying, "I'm sorry, sir. I have strict orders that no one is to remove the list. You'll have to put it back." The CEO glared at her for a minute and then asked, "Do you know who I am?" She replied that she didn't, but that no one was permitted to look at the log. The executive replied, "Well, when you pick up your *final* paycheck this afternoon, ask them to tell you."

As a large group, we discuss how Leonard puts his values into practice and in creating this list also see what actions we could take to put our own values into practice. We know the meaning of DWYSYWD (which is embossed on our seminar pens): Do What You Say You Will Do.

From modeling, we move on to the fifth practice, "Encouraging the Heart." We go back to the film *In Search of Excellence* and watch a segment on Tom Melohn, the CEO of a tool and die company. He demonstrates in his behavior and attitude a deep sense of caring for his employees. This module focuses on how leaders reward and celebrate the accomplishments of their people and their organization. We as a group brainstorm out a list of ways to recognize others and celebrate accomplishments by (1) setting high standards, (2) catching people doing things right, (3) being creative with rewards, (4) recognizing others in public, (5) personalizing rewards, (6) telling the story, and (7) repeating the standard. This brings us to the end of the day and to preparation for our final day's activity, making commitments.

As homework, we are given a commitment exercise in which we must answer a series of questions concerning what new challenges we want to set up for ourselves. For example, we are asked, "What challenging opportunities—new experiences, job assignments, tasks—can you seek to test your skills and abilities?" "What can you do to challenge the way things are done—the status quo—at work?" "Where can you experiment and take risks with new approaches to your work even when there is a chance you might fail?" "What can you do to improve your abilities to envision an uplifting and ennobling future?" Several pages of questions like these and a "commitment memo" will be our homework.

The commitment memo is the course's mechanism for ensuring back-home follow-up on what we have been learning. We are asked to select one of our fellow participants to be our partner over the next three weeks. Our partner will support us as a consultant. Partners will help by offering advice, encouragement, or feedback. We in turn will do the same for our partner. On the memo, we outline actions that we will take over the next three weeks to help create the future we wish to envision. The idea is that we will give each other duplicates of our commitment memo and then mail them out to each other in three weeks to see how well we have followed up. While I thought this was a useful idea, I found that the majority of participants did not follow up, for various reasons. Again, this evening, after dinner, we are invited to see the videotape of today's outdoor activities.

The final day is spent reviewing our visions and preparing a five-minute "stump speech," which we must give to members of a five-person team. The idea is that our speeches will be inspiring in both style and content, and will be directly related to our vision for our work. Everyone prepares diligently, and, surprisingly, most of our speeches are relatively inspiring. We then give each other feedback on our presentations, as to their strengths and weaknesses. We also provide feedback on any other things (actions, ideas, comments) we have observed about one another and appreciated. Our final assignment is to plan, in small groups, celebration activities for the closing session of the seminar. The course comes to a close with each group's presentation. They range from parodies of Jim and Barry, a Leadership Challenge version of the television show "Jeopardy," and a poem to a rap song about leaders. Jim and Barry award each participant a certificate and seminar mementos, and say a word or two about the person's contribution to this leadership adventure. We laugh, shed a few tears, and clap and cheer before a final "bon voyage" toast is offered.

Chapter Six

Looking into the Mirror: The Feedback Approaches

*F*eedback refers to the process of giving someone accurate information about the impact of his or her behavior on you, other people, and/or the completion of a task.

We give feedback all the time — as managers, as parents, as spouses, as friends, as co-workers. Feedback is the method we use to change behavior, improve performance, deal with stress, and enrich relationships.

To be constructive, feedback should be intended to (a) motivate the receiver to continue effective behavior, or (b) supply information that will help solve a problem, or (c) enable the person to become more productive. Only when the intention is to be helpful, and that information is communicated, will the recipient be likely to accept the information and use it in a positive manner.

                — Center for Creative Leadership

The third of our four training approaches to leadership development puts its primary emphasis on feedback. It assumes that most of us already have some form of leadership style, and that through feedback we can learn what the strengths and pitfalls of that particular style are. Armed with this information, par-

Epigraph from the Center for Creative Leadership, copyright 1988. Reprinted with permission.

ticipants can return to the job to amend their weaknesses and act in confidence, knowing their strengths.

One of the most outstanding examples of a feedback-oriented program is the Leadership Development Program at the Center for Creative Leadership in Greensboro, North Carolina. The Center itself is a nonprofit, educational institution founded in 1970, with a mission to encourage and develop creative leadership for the good of society. In addition to the training that goes on there, the Center sponsors an active research group of social scientists looking at issues of leadership, creativity, and the management of change.

One of the Center's principal programs is the Leadership Development Program. Offered more than 150 times in 1990 alone, this program emphasizes assessment and constructive feedback in both management and leadership behavior, using a combination of tests, surveys, assessment exercises, simulations, and lectures. Participants average forty-two years of age and fifteen years of work experience. Some 69 percent are from business backgrounds (largely Fortune 500 companies), and the rest are from nonprofit organizations or the government and military. The program is largely the brainchild of its director, Bob Dorn, who conceived and developed the first presentation, in 1974, with a group of Center staff members.[1]

As a result of his work in psychiatric hospitals and with the Peace Corps, Bob had become aware of the important role that feedback could play in helping people achieve personal growth and development. After several years of establishing and directing assessment centers for the Peace Corps, Bob joined the Center for Creative Leadership in 1969. Bringing with him expertise in assessment and an interest in training and development, he initiated a series of weekend self-development programs for undergraduate students from nearby universities. These were designed for the students to examine their own behavior and its impact on others. From these early programs Bob formulated what later became the Leadership Development Program. The program's design was guided (and still is guided) by three elements and the characteristic principles behind them: the training philosophy ("effective leadership development begins

with assessment by self and others and with constructive feedback"); the program objectives ("interactive experiences where
participants learn from each other"); and intended outcomes
("to help the individual become more productive and happier
and, as a leader, to help others achieve these same goals").[2]

The Leadership Development Program

Several weeks before beginning the program, I receive a package stuffed with tests and questionnaires to fill out. An accompanying letter welcomes me to the program and alerts
me to the six to eight hours of "homework" I must complete
before my arrival. As well, I must give copies of the various
forms to superiors, peers, and subordinates to fill out on my
behavior. This is a hint of the extent of feedback that is to
come over the six-day program (Exhibits 6.1 and 6.2 outline
the course).

On the first day of the course I observe a wide range of
ages and professions among the participants; some are from
profit and some from nonprofit organizations, though most are
middle managers. From informal discussions, I learn that the
majority of my fellow participants are here thanks to a "mis-
sionary" manager who has been through the course and has encouraged them to attend.

As we settle into our chairs around a large U-shaped table,
our instructors inform us that the course will help us to become
more successful in both our personal and professional lives, and
help us to lead others to becoming more successful. Specifically,
we are going to examine the process of "creative" leadership,
of self-growth and development, and how we can continue these
processes for the rest of our lives. But, as it turns out, feedback
will be the main theme throughout the course.

We begin this Sunday afternoon by receiving bibs, each
with a Greek letter boldly printed on it. Mine is Zeta. Each participant has a different letter. In addition, with each bib we
receive a set of instructions, which in my case read as follows:

Exhibit 6.1. Leadership Development Program Daily Schedule.

	Sunday	Monday	Tuesday	Wednesday	Thursday	Friday
7:30 A.M.			BREAKFAST AT 7:45 A.M.			
Morning (8:15 A.M.)		The Creative Leadership Process	Decision Making — When to use a group	Factors of Executive Success	Feedback — • Staff • Peer	Preparation for Goal Setting — Goal Setting
12:00			LUNCH			
Afternoon	Program Opening — Introductions — Assessment Activities	Performance Development	Utilizing Group Resources — How to use a group	Interviews — Presentation on Feedback — 2:30 Free Time	Feedback — • Staff • Peer	Goal Setting (continued) — Final Evaluations — Program Close 1:00 P.M.
Evening (5:30 P.M.)	DINNER	DINNER	DINNER		Banquet Off-site	

Source: Center for Creative Leadership, copyright 1990. Reprinted with permission.

Exhibit 6.2. Leadership Development
Program Component Overview.

The Creative Leadership Process	Monday Morning

Model: The Eight Phases of Creative Leadership: Assessment, Formulation, Transformation, Goal Setting, Planning and Organizing, Implementation, Evaluation/Control, Reassessment
Exercise: The Hollow Square [a puzzle assembled by a planning team and
an implementing team]; Planning & Implementing Exercise
Feedback: Kirton Adaption–Innovation Inventory [KAI, a view of problem-
solving styles ranging from Adaptive (A) to Innovative (I)]

Performance Development	Monday Afternoon

Model: Performance Development: Leader behavior [S-1/Structuring,
S-2/Coaching, S-3/Encouraging, S-4/Delegating], a function of
the task and the subordinate's performance level [P-1 to P-4],
as determined by skill, motivation, and responsibility
Exercise: Situational Leadership Game
Feedback: Leadership Style Indicator [LSI], completed by you and by up
to six subordinates or peers, on perceptions of your leadership
style [S-1 to S-4] and effectiveness [ratios of 0.00 to 1.00, along
with "Be More/Be Less" advice]
Activity: Development by Objectives (DBO)

Decision Making	Tuesday Morning

Model: When and how to involve others [L1, L2, LF1, LF2, M] in decision making, as determined by Quality, Acceptance, and Time
Exercise: Applying the model, in small groups, to several of the sixteen
cases in the Leadership Decision Styles Survey [LDSS]
Feedback: Myers-Briggs Type Indicator [MBTI]
Leadership Decision Styles Survey [LDSS printout summariz-
ing your preprogram responses to the sixteen cases]

Utilizing Group Resources	Tuesday Afternoon

Model: The Creative Leadership Window: achieving synergy in groups
through the effective use of twelve task and relationship behaviors
that enlarge the "Arena" by decreasing the "Mask" and "Blind-
spot" and thus tap into "Potential Creativity"
Exercise: Project Planning Exercise, first done alone and then in a small
group and videotaped
Feedback: Review of videotape, followed by giving and receiving feedback
from other group members

Exhibit 6.2. Leadership Development
Program Component Overview, Cont'd.

Factors of Executive Success   Wednesday Morning

Presentation: The Center's two-year study on factors predictive of executive
                 success and derailment
Feedback: Management Skills Profile [MSP], completed by you, superiors,
                 subordinates, and peers, giving you scores on eighteen different
                 management skills

Peer and Staff Feedback   Thursday

Peer: Participants give feedback to one another on the effects of their
                 behavior during the program
Staff: A confidential two- to three-hour session with a professional CCL
                 consultant to review and discuss all the test and behavioral data
                 collected prior to and during the program

Goal Setting   Friday

Presentation: Goal clarity and motivation as key elements necessary for suc-
                 cessfully attaining one's goals; the Button-Button as a symbol
                 of the four key areas in one's life — Career, Family, Community,
                 and Personal
Individual
Goal Setting: A variety of individual and small-group activities that help par-
                 ticipants focus on how they can apply what they have learned
                 during the week by setting concrete, meaningful, and attainable
                 goals

Source: Center for Creative Leadership, copyright 1991. Reprinted with
permission.

Jay Conger (Zeta)
You will be observing and giving
feedback to:
John Donovan (Nu) and Andrew Cutler (Omicron)

You are also responsible for gathering
information on:
Ann Karens (Beta)
Bill Eaton (Omega)
Sally Thorton (Delta)

These are the individuals (whose names I have disguised) whom I will be observing throughout the week and ultimately will be responsible for giving candid feedback about their behavior during the seminar. With our instructions, we are given peer feedback sheets on which to record our observations (Exhibit 6.3). We are then told that all the feedback we give to our assigned partners will be filtered through group observations. This is to ensure consensus on each point of behavioral feedback. My observation partners will not even see the individual feedback sheets that I fill out on them. At this point, the staff emphasizes strongly the confidentiality of the entire process for each of us.

Before moving to our first group exercise, we are given a test called the Hidden Figures test, which looks at problem-solving skills. This is the first of several tests we will complete during the program at seemingly random times. Again, the idea is to provide each participant with a wide range of feedback perspectives on personality, management style, leadership style, decision-making style, and so on.

We begin the group exercise, which is entitled Earth II. We each receive a manual explaining that a planet has been discovered that is similar to Earth, with the exception that there are no forms of intelligent life on it. An unmanned space probe discovered the planet in A.D. 2044, and scientists explored it in A.D. 2045. Earth, meanwhile, is in a crisis because of overpopulation and pollution. A decision has been made by the governments of the earth to send 0.1 percent of the world's population to start anew on Earth II.

There are technological problems, however. A colossal space ship is needed, and because of the enormous resources required, only one can be built. Once there, it will be dismantled and used in constructing the new settlement. The only dilemma is that a small star will soon move between Earth and Earth II and become a supernova. As a result, space travel between the two planets will be cut off for two hundred years.

There are also human problems. Since only 0.1 percent of the earth's population can go, who will be chosen? Eventually, it is decided that the settlers will be chosen by lot, and each

Exhibit 6.3. Behavioral Examples for Peer Feedback.

	Situation	Behavior	Impact on You	Perceived Impact on Others and/or the Task
Example 1	When we were gathering before the program began.	Alpha walked over and introduced herself.	Made me feel comfortable and included.	
Example 2	Earth II	Presentation was concise and to the point but without much enthusiasm.	Felt Alpha didn't really believe her candidate was best for the position.	Others seemed to dismiss Alpha's candidate as a contender and focused on two other candidates.
Example 3	Earth II	Alpha was quiet; did little to support or promote her candidate.	Wondered about her apparent lack of interest in accomplishing the task.	Did not contribute as a team member— did little to help us get the job done.

Source: Center for Creative Leadership, copyright 1988. Reprinted with permission.

nation will send 0.1 percent of its population. If an individual is chosen who has a family, the family will automatically be included.

Our task in this exercise is to serve on the leader selection committee. Prior to the gathering of the committee (which is about to happen), each member has reviewed the résumés of several hundred individuals who were nominated as candidates to lead the expedition. The committee has narrowed those to be interviewed down to five (the number of people in our team). Now we, as a committee, must select one person to be the project leader.

We are instructed that our task as individuals is twofold: (1) We are to fill out a résumé form on the fictitious individual we feel would be best qualified to be the leader, so we must make up the characteristics and experiences that qualify this person to be the leader of Earth II. (2) We are to prepare a presentation that will convince our committee members that our person is the best choice, emphasizing our candidate's greatest accomplishments.

The résumé forms require information in areas such as the candidate's nationality, sex, age, status, education, work experience, job, employer, and so on. Essentially, each of us writes up a résumé of our ideal applicant, and then we debate among ourselves to determine whose ideal will make the best candidate. At the end of a half hour, we must reach a consensus with a rank ordering of our preferred candidates.

Our group produces a lively debate. In the last few minutes, we finally reach a consensus, but only after a good deal of politicking and persuading. My candidate is ranked second; the one ranked first is that of a very persuasive young manager.

I am reminded by this exercise of the importance of subtlety in influencing others, especially peers. One individual fought so hard for his candidate that he lost our support immediately. Persuasion has to be artful. As well, at one point, the group dissolved into anarchy as each member clung tightly to his or her candidate. A consensus seemed impossible at that moment. A minute later, a few of us recognized the stalemate we had created and moved to entertain more seriously other viewpoints in order to reach a consensus. In a funny way, "leadership" in this exercise took the forms of maturely giving in to a well-reasoned argument as well as presenting one.

When we complete the exercise, we rate each other on feedback forms. In addition, many or our exercises are conducted in rooms fitted with one-way mirrors behind which psychologists on the staff of the Center for Creative Leadership rank us along the same dimensions as our peers. These dimensions include (1) level of activity in the group, (2) leading the discussion, (3) influencing others, (4) problem analysis, (5) task orientation, (6) motivating others, (7) interpersonal skills, and (8) verbal effectiveness. Several days later, we will receive our ratings, but for now, we have no idea how well we have done, other than by the number of votes our candidate receives.

We have one final group exercise before dinner called Energy International (which is from the 1972 Annual Handbook for Group Facilitators, revised 1986 edition). In groups of six, we must choose one candidate from among eleven for a position at the fictitious company Energy International. We are given eleven résumés as well as a sheet outlining the ideal background of the type of candidate we need. While the exercise sounds simple enough, we quickly discover that each of the individual booklets of résumés is different from the others. So the process becomes one of teamwork, searching to piece together our different bits of information. Again, we are given a time limit, and we present our solution at the end. Afterward, we are ranked by our team members and the staff psychologists behind the mirror on the eight dimensions used in Earth II. Our group proceeds very cooperatively and soon completes the exercise successfully. We learn later that other teams were more competitive among their members and as a result were less successful.

Energy International is used to illustrate ideas about cooperation in a group and the effective sharing of information. It is particularly effective for individuals who normally turn a cooperative effort into a competitive one; they are able to see quite clearly their tendency to do this even in a situation like this, where it is not constructive. Earth II, in contrast, measures individuals' presentation and persuasion skills. Both are helpful in highlighting team leaders who are effective through influence skills.

The second day of the program starts with an exercise in which a ball is handed to one of the twenty-five participants, and we then each hand it off to the person next to us. We are asked to remember who gave us the ball and to whom we gave it. We are also timed to see how long it takes. The process begins over again; this time, we are told we must complete the handoff in half the original time. There is only one rule: the ball must touch everyone's hand. We finish, and within our time limit. The game continues, and with each new round, the time is halved. Our group finally reaches a point where we have only a matter of seconds in which to pass the ball among twenty-five people — a seemingly impossible task. With some brainstorming, we figure out that the first person can simply run around the group touching each person's hands if we place them all in the correct order. We do, and we succeed. The exercise nicely demonstrates ideas of group brainstorming, a willingness to challenge assumptions, and shared leadership. But most of all, I am reminded, as in the previous exercise, of the camaraderie of positive teamwork.

After this, we focus on leadership. Working in small groups, we are asked to come up with a single-sentence definition of a leader. We are given ten minutes to do this. This begins our morning session, whose theme is "The Creative Leadership Process." In this exercise, it becomes clear that most of us have read the current literature on leadership, as words like "vision" and "empowerment" are immediately bantered about. Yet, at the same time, there is a fair amount of debate as we attempt to distinguish between a leader and a manager. Each team reports its definition back to the entire group. The facilitator then offers the Center's definition of a leader. Four qualities are described: (1) Vision — conceiving a desirable and achievable goal; (2) Communication — presenting ideas in a way that subordinates understand and are willing to align themselves with; (3) Empowerment — motivating subordinates to participate; and (4) Action — taking action and allowing others to act. A written definition of the creative leader is given to us: "The task of the creative leader is to envision and bring about changes which have beneficial long-term consequences not only for his or her part of the organization but for the organization as a whole and the total society of which that organization is a part. An inseparable part of this mission is to help each individual in the organization develop his or her full potential, not only as a contributing member but as a unique human being."

A debate ensues about the definition and the idea of empowerment. It proves an interesting discussion, but it opens up challenges to the Center's definition. An additional problem is that the definition is quite humanistic — after all the Center is staffed largely by psychologists, not business people — and participants challenge the idealism.

By midmorning, we are in debate about the differences between managers and leaders. John Kotter's material on the differences between the two is used, as well as an eight-phase model developed by the Center (Figure 6.1). Like hands on a clock, the discussion of the model moves around each of the eight phases. We begin with the "Formulation" (vision) phase of the Center's model. The work of psychologist Clay Alderfer is introduced: his model of human needs. His three need categories — existence, growth, and relationships — are outlined, and our trainer discusses how the goals we envision must address these needs to have maximum appeal for subordinates. Alderfer's need categories are then tied into a discussion of power. While this is all useful information, the class does not seem to connect well to the material; it seems too abstract for many of the participants.

We move to the "Transformation" phase of the Center's model. To illustrate our own inclinations toward being more transformational, we are given the results of an inventory we have completed prior to the program, called the Kirton Adaptation–Innovation Inventory. This instrument is timed for this section because it describes one's inclination toward the status quo or toward change. As it turns out, I find that I am strongly oriented toward change, whereupon my interest in the model picks up. We now have some sense of where we stand individually on this dimension of the program's leadership model.

Figure 6.1. Eight Phases of Creative Leadership.

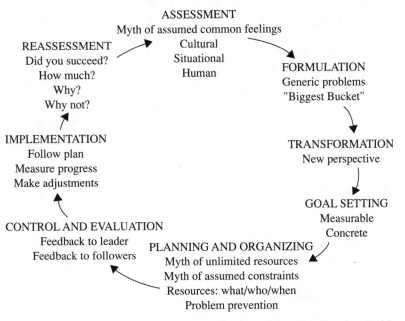

Source: Center for Creative Leadership. Copyright 1976. Reprinted with permission.

"Goal setting" is the next phase, and it involves a model that seems too complex to hold the attention of most partici- pants. I am quickly reminded that effective management train- ing in these contexts demands simple yet memorable models that ensure impact and retention. If it were not for the fact that we have several days of information to go and are sometimes in our seats for hours at a time, we might remember the model.

After fifteen minutes, we move on to the "Planning and Organizing" phase. To ground ourselves in its basic ideas, we perform an exercise that reveals how planning departments and implementing departments do not cooperate.[3] Each team is divided into two groups, the planners and the implementors. The groups are separated in the beginning and given different instructions. The implementors are not told the result of the process; only the planners know this information. The exercise centers on a wooden puzzle that has a hollow center; the implementors must piece it together correctly with the assistance of the planners.

This is a wonderfully playful exercise that clearly exemplifies the dynamics between planners and implementors: there are moments of poor communication, bad feelings, and so on. Our team masters the exercise, while the other team fails because of a complete lack of communication between the planners and the implementors. This is a powerful illustration of the "Planning and Organizing" phase, and effectively teaches the value of participation and information sharing. Like the Kirton Inventory during the transformation discussion, the exercise helps ground the ideas in the model.

We move quickly through the next element of the model, "Control and Evaluation," and then on to the remaining two, "Implementation" and "Reassessment." Little time is spent on these because the Center contends that often too much attention is devoted to these in training. This is perhaps the result of some bias toward the implicit assumption that the right-hand side of the phase model reflects more the skills of the innovative leader, whereas the left-hand dimensions of control and reassessment are more reflective of managerial and adaptive functions. We learn, for example, that the right side of the model (as you face it) reflects Kirton's Innovators, while the left reflects Kirton's Adaptors. Both types are derived from the Kirton Adaptation–Innovation Inventory, which we were tested on earlier. The Kirton Adaptors are individuals who seek to improve things within existing approaches, whereas the Innovators seek solutions that do things differently. The Adaptors prefer well-established and structured situations, while the Innovators prefer unstructured situations.

Following lunch, we are introduced to the Creative Leadership Model, which is derived from the Ohio State research studies of the 1950s. Essentially, it is a typology of four leadership styles: encouraging, coaching, delegating, and structuring (Figure 6.2). We will spend most of the rest of the day examining this model through exercises and the Leadership Style Inventory (LSI), a feedback instrument. Our facilitator will then

Figure 6.2. LSI Summary Report.

Encouraging Style (S-3)	Coaching Style (S-2)
Delegating Style (S-4)	Structuring Style (S-1)

Relationship Behavior

Task Behavior

Source: Center for Creative Leadership. Copyright 1988. Reprinted with permission.

tie the model to the performance levels of our subordinates. For example, he explains that if we have a subordinate who is underperforming at a task, the person may require more structuring leadership on our part, whereas if the subordinate is performing significantly above expectations, he or she may need more delegating leadership.[4]

To ground the basic ideas further, we play a game that illustrates when to use each of the four leadership styles. We divide into teams to compete against each other. In the front of the room is a flip chart with what is the equivalent of a board game drawn on it. It consists of a pathway undulating past numbered blocks. Each team tries to move along these blocks, with the winner being the first to arrive at the end. When we land on a block, we are given a scenario for which we must pick the correct leadership style. If we choose correctly, a colored pin representing our team is moved ahead two spaces. If we choose incorrectly, we must go back one or two spaces, depending on how wrong we are. The trainers have the correct answers. Using play to illustrate the model appears to be enjoyed by all and is a useful way to teach the theory. There is plenty of laughter and rivalry. Initially, I was concerned that the model might be too dated; yet for midlevel managers (most of the participants), it seems appropriate since the delegation/participation issue is very much a part of managing at this level.

After the game, we are given the results of our work on the Leadership Style Inventory. It turns out that coaching is my primary style. I am not surprised, given that I am a teacher and spend much of my time "coaching" students. I notice with all the feedback tests that I examine my negatives first, especially those that are strongly negative. I discover that I am a bit too independent, analytical, and reflective in my leadership style. Our scores are displayed on the classroom wall without our names being disclosed, and in this way, we are able to see how we stand relative to one another.

For the next day, decision making is our focus. We expand on the previous day's discussion by looking at five decision/participation categories. These are (1) we make the decision alone (denoted L1); (2) we seek further information from one or more subordinates but do not share the problem with them (L2); (3) we consult with selected individuals, share the problem, and gather additional information from them (LF1); (4) we bring the entire group together and discuss alternative solutions, but we make the final decision (LF2); and (5) we share the problem with the group, and the group makes the decision (M). The facilitator explains that the time required to make a decision increases as we progress from L1 to M, but that acceptance by subordinates also increases from L1 to M. We are given handouts that explain in more detail these various options and where they are most effectively employed. Prior to the course, we have taken a test on this material to determine our inclinations among these five approaches. When we receive our results, I discover that I use the participative styles too often and in situations where they are not necessary.

We shift to a questionnaire on decision making, which we have completed prior to taking the course: the Myers-Briggs

Type Indicator (MBTI). (I assume that readers are familiar with this instrument, so I will not go into detail about it.) There is some overlap between the MBTI and the Leadership Style Indicator, and in class an attempt is made to link the two. This effort is only partially successful because on several dimensions the two approaches concern themselves with different aspects of decision making.

After we receive our Myers-Briggs results, we return to the Leadership Style Indicator for another game. Four scenarios are chosen for which, working in teams, we must choose the correct decision-making approach. We have twenty minutes to come up with out answers, which will be listed on a flip chart showing each team's choice for the various scenarios. Following this, we are presented with results from a similar exercise that we completed prior to taking the course. This particular practice of introducing a model, using a problem-solving game or exercise to illustrate it, and then providing individual feedback from tests taken before the course appears to be effective, given participants' reactions.

That afternoon, the Creative Leadership Window (Figure 6.3) is used to introduce the issue of information and who has it. We determine that certain task- and people-oriented leadership behaviors are more appropriate than others, depending on the extent to which information is held by the leader or others. We then go to a group decision-making exercise (similar to the well-known NASA Moon or Nuclear Survival exercises) involving a research and development scenario in which we, as a team, must rank-order our priorities. It is called the Project Planning exercise, and it is designed to illustrate group decision-making processes when the information given is limited. The process is videotaped, and for the remainder of the afternoon we give feedback to one another on our behavior in the group. A round-robin procedure is used for feedback so that each of us is assured of our fair share of it. Most of what we have been learning so far has focused on leading teams, with a special emphasis on decision-making styles.

Wednesday is spent learning about the Center's study on executive success and derailment. Other times, this module may

Figure 6.3. Creative Leadership Window.

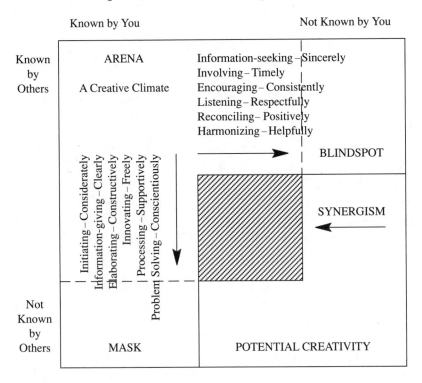

Source: Center for Creative Leadership. Copyright 1988. Adapted from the Johari Window concept developed by Joe Luft and Harry Ingham. Reprinted with permission.

be "lessons of experience" or "learning to learn" from research by the Center's staff on executive development. The idea is simply to help participants think ahead about the factors that will help or hinder them in their careers.

For the remainder of the day, we focus on feedback from an instrument we have completed prior to the course called the Management Skills Profile (MSP). This is an expensive and somewhat lengthy test that we have also given to our superiors, peers, and subordinates. The range of skill categories it covers is comprehensive, although the emphasis is on management skills (that is, informing, listening, oral and written communications, conflict management, delegating, coaching, planning, organizing, personal motivation, occupational knowledge, time management) rather than what we would call leadership skills. We review our results individually and then share in small groups. We also act as consultants for one another on areas of development, and we draw up a list of development priorities. I, for example, need to work more on conflict management, overcome a need to be liked, take more risks with voicing my stand, and so on. At this point, I am beginning to feel a state of "test overload"; we have results now from numerous tests, and it is increasingly difficult to remember what to focus on for personal development. The irony is that the feedback process has only begun. Tomorrow we face an entire day devoted to staff and peer feedback.

Thursday we begin our course of intensive feedback by joining groups of three other participants who have been assigned either the same primary or secondary people to observe. (You will remember that on the first day I was given the names of two individuals to watch most closely — the primary — and three individuals less closely — the secondary.) We solicit from our group as much feedback as possible on our primary person. We then develop a consensus around our own observations and the group's — this will be the information we feed back. In this way, our own biases are largely filtered out. We role-play with the group how we will deliver our feedback to the primary individual so that we have a chance to carefully rehearse what we have to say.

One of my primary individuals is a tough one. In Earth II, he has been dogmatic and overpowering. In the next exercise, he was so caught up in his own perspective that he could not pay attention to others' comments. Later, he would make several demeaning comments to fellow participants. Yet, underneath this I suspected there was quite a good human being who had somehow become highly insecure. The group is helpful in putting together useful feedback for him.

This process takes a group of four approximately two hours; it is a highly effective means of delivering accurate feedback. In addition, the Center has a very useful mechanism for additional feedback if you wish it. There is a feedback sheet that we can hand in to our facilitator to request feedback on a particular aspect of our behavior. Our peer observer will then make a point of noting that behavior.

I learn from my peers that I am easygoing, strong in social skills, a bit unconventional in a positive manner, sometimes too analytical, and occasionally willing to compromise too quickly. My troublesome primary individual listens intently to his feedback and suddenly softens, explaining difficulties in his personal life that have recently hardened him.

The afternoon is spent one-on-one in a confidential, two-to three-hour session with a staff psychologist to review and discuss all the test and behavioral data collected prior to and during the program. This session is rated by participants as the highlight of the entire week, and from my own experience, I would agree. It is an opportunity to pull together what one has been learning. In addition, feedback from the staff member has an air of credibility that that of peers does not always possess. Most important, the staff member is able to show how the tests link to one another and to summarize strengths and areas of development. For me, it is the statement of my strengths that stands out and that surprises me. Normally a tough critic of myself, I learn to my shock that I have leadership talent — at least according to the CCL staff! For example, in the Earth II and Energy International exercises, I have been ranked first in effectiveness. Yet, the paradox is that group members ranked me either second or third. I wonder why I have not been able to manage the same impression with the two groups. It sparks thoughts about whether I am using my abilities fully.

Friday, the final day, is devoted to goal setting. Our facilitator begins this module by talking about the results of research on successful executives conducted by the Center. He highlights the fact that they are persistent in striving toward their goals. Persistence, he argues, comes when the goals we are pursuing are consistent with what we believe and want. The problem, however, is that very few of us know the goals we want. Using a button as a metaphor, he tells us that we will examine the four areas of our life (like the four holes in a button) where goals are important for our well-being and effectiveness. The four areas are personal, community, family, and career.

For each of these four areas, we are instructed to write down twenty things we enjoy doing. So, for example, for the personal area, I write *reading, swimming, listening to music, talking with friends,* and so on. After completing our list, we go back over each item and ask ourselves, "Would I enjoy doing that more if I could do it better?" If yes, then we are to write the phrase *more skill needed* next to it. After this, we ask ourselves, "Would I like to spend more time doing this than I do?" If so, we write *time* next to the corresponding item. We go through the list one last time asking ourselves, "How would I rank order each of these in terms of which in my life is the most enjoyable, second most enjoyable, third . . . and so on?" The idea, or course, is to force participants to reflect on any discrepancies between what they are doing and what they wish they were doing. After we work through a topic area, we discuss our findings in small groups, and particularly the surprises.

Under the topic of family, we are asked to think of all the people who love us and whom we love. This becomes quite powerful as we realize that there are only a handful of people who fit into this category. The question we ask ourselves about each person on our list is, "Is there anything I could be doing for this person that would increase or improve this relationship?"

In the career area, these questions are posed: "How are we developing our people?" "Are we committed to it?" We then go on to the community. These last two categories do not receive the same degree of attention as the first two did. It seems clear that the group is more interested in the first two. The connection of this exercise to leadership on the job is indirect; many of our goals are personal, that is, they exist outside of work. All of this is leading to a final exercise in which we map out four important future goals for ourselves, relative to any of the four areas we have been reviewing. We work with one or two other individuals to refine our goals, though some of us choose to do this alone. I devise the following as my goals: (1) to spend more time in Montreal and less time traveling, (2) to exercise a minimum of four times a week, (3) to spend more time on my personal relationships, and (4) to focus longer term on career plans.

We each write our four goals onto a goal report form (Exhibit 6.4), which we leave with the Center to be mailed to us at some point in the near future (say, in three months). Once we receive it, we are to check whether we have completed, are still in progress on, or have dropped our goals. The idea is that this will help maintain our momentum in working seriously on our individual goals. The program closes with a round of hand-shakes and hugs. We bid goodbye to each other and head off to vans waiting to take us to the airport.

Exhibit 6.4. Goal Report Form.

Name: _____   Today's Date: _____

Address: _____

_____   *CONTACT

_____   DATE: _____

Phone: _____

For report purposes: If goal is not worked on within two weeks of contact,
and has not been completed, mark DROPPED.

Type of Goal Personal Career Family Community	COMPLETED	IN PROCESS	DROPPED	Goal Statement
				#1

Comments:

				#2

Comments:

				#3

Comments:

				#4

Comments:

*Please fill in CONTACT DATE at top of page.

Chapter Seven

Mastering the Zen of Leadership: The Skill-Building Approaches

When you sit down to practice [Zen] you will almost certainly find that your mind is in a condition like boiling water: restless impulses push up inside you, and wandering thoughts jostle at the door of consciousness. . . . The important thing is to stop the first thought. . . . The first stage of practice, then, is solely dedicated to checking wandering thoughts. Breathing at this stage is done with the mouth slightly open; the breath is forced out through the narrow gap between the lips. . . . As we do this we say inwardly, "Mu . . . Mu . . . Mu . . . " The abdomen will cave in by degrees, but do not allow the lowest part of the abdomen to cave in completely. Exhale until the reserve volume is almost expired. Then inflate the bottom of the abdomen and begin inhalation.

— Katsuki Sekida

This chapter's opening quotation is from the book *Zen Training,* published in 1977 and the first self-instruction manual on Zen available in North America. In it, the Zen teacher Sekida outlines very specific steps to becoming a Zen master. At the time the book was published, Sekida's approach was considered quite extraordinary; Zen was considered a relatively mystifying religious practice. Zen masters, like leaders, were accorded the status of special individuals. The notion that one could simply follow a series of instructions to learn the skills of a Zen master was almost heretical. Yet the book's author succeeded in demystifying the practice into a set of specific instructions so that you and I as individuals could learn Zen. The skill-building approaches to leadership development assume, similarly, that through a series of step-by-step instructions and demonstrations managers can learn the skills and techniques of leaders. They assume that leadership can be demystified and translated into discrete skills, like Zen practices.

Of all the approaches to leadership training, the skills-oriented approaches have the oldest history. Training in leadership skills began with the simple task-versus-people skills identified by researchers in the 1950s and 1960s. Because of their simplicity, these earlier models lent themselves well to skill-building exercises. But, as interest has shifted to leadership at more senior levels of organizations, the question of how to teach such complex forms of leadership is a more difficult one to answer. Nonetheless, programs have appeared that assert their ability to teach people some of these more complicated skills.

The Forum Company, headquartered in Boston, Massachusetts, has designed one of the most popular of these skills courses, and it is their program, entitled "Leadership," that my research assistant and I investigated. Their program will serve as an example of the skills orientation to leadership training.

Formed in 1971 and employing over three hundred individuals, the Forum Company is a training and consulting firm that focuses on five areas of expertise: establishing customer-focused quality, increasing sales productivity, developing leadership and managerial effectiveness, fostering innovation, and shaping corporate culture to facilitate strategic change. It offers a wide array of training programs, only one of which is on leadership. The firm is unique in its orientation to research and its compilation of a database of business practices; for more than twenty years it has collected data on organizational and individual competencies from its wide range of clients. So, for example, managers on a sales training program can have their sales competencies rated against managers in the same or other industries and against thousands of other managers who have participated in Forum programs.

Early research design for the Leadership Course was based upon work at Harvard Business School, which demonstrated the links between organizational climate and individual motivation. Forum developed that work in the late 1970s to show how managers could have effective influence across organizational lines. In designing and conducting customized leadership training courses for Fortune 500 firms, it began to build a research-based body of knowledge on leadership.

In the late 1980s, Forum decided to consolidate its experience and research in leadership into a standard course that could be delivered to mid- to senior-level managers around the world. A large research project was conducted, involving 93 managers and 492 associates in seven major service and manufacturing corporations. This research project differed from other leadership studies in that the conclusions were derived from the reports of the associates rather than from self-reports.

Forum's research showed how many of the interdependent practices of leadership, such as developing other people's talents, caring for others, and including others in decision making, are highly correlated with the perception of effective leadership. This work served as the basis for the current program model, which teaches managers how to be leaders in their work units and organizations. It also provided the basis for a feedback instrument that is administered to participants prior to their entry into the program.

The development of the research and the program was done by a team with members that cut across all departments, including research, product development, marketing, and instruction. There were literally dozens of people who played a role in the leadership research and program development. Many diverse talents and backgrounds came together to ensure that the final program would be applicable to managers in all types of situations, in organizations around the world.

The following description of the Leadership Course is derived from my research assistant Ann Latimer's experiences in it.

Introduction to Forum's Leadership Course

Nine of us are sitting at desks arranged in a U-shape. Diane, our instructor, is at the center with three flip charts. Diane (her real name) is a Harvard MBA and an executive vice president at Forum. She outlines our goals for the week: to improve our understanding of leadership; to learn which leadership practices are critical in our environment; to practice some old and new ways of leading; and to focus on critical actions we can take. Diane runs through these quickly and then shows us a five-minute video of children defining leadership. We are asked to think about what leadership means to us, as we watch the video. The general consensus is that the kids understand perfectly well what leadership is all about — that even at an early age we have an appreciation for its role in society.

We open the first of several booklets prepared for the program by the Forum and spend five minutes on an individual exercise on leadership beliefs. We are given sixteen leadership statements, and out of these we are asked to pick the three that mean the most to us. Once we have done this, we circulate among ourselves and divide into small groups with others who have chosen the same statements.

I opt for "leaders listen," which, as it turns out, just about everyone picks. My next choice, "there are two ways of exerting one's strength: one is pushing down, the other is pulling up," is generally unpopular; all of my classmates frown on the notion of "exerting one's strength" — which, perhaps unfortunately for me, is something I tend to like to do. My third choice is "I am not suggesting that good leaders are necessarily nice, understanding human beings. Some of the best I have known have been truculent, difficult people — but they are committed. They meant what they said. They cared." I like this one's emphasis on commitment and caring, and a few of my classmates agree with me.

Most popular with others are the following two statements: "The signs of outstanding leadership appear primarily among the followers. Are the followers reaching their potential? Are they learning? Serving? Do they achieve the required results? Do they change with grace? Manage conflict?" and "Time is neutral and does not change things. With courage and initiative, leaders change things." Diane lists the characteristics we find important in a leader:

- staying in touch
- caring
- listening
- having vision
- understanding
- feeling responsible
- taking initiative
- empowering
- having courage
- encouraging risk taking
- not being concerned about failure

Diane then describes the research on which Forum's leadership course is based. The research for the seminar was built on a database drawn from Forum's custom-based training experience since 1982. It was expanded with a survey of seven hundred executives, input from focus groups that represented the audience, and literature reviews. The result was eighty-six practices. Using a review board of middle to senior management, Forum narrowed the practices down to the forty-six considered most important, and conducted a final validation of the practices that reduced the number to twenty.[1]

We are presented with Forum's leadership model, symbolized by their logo, puzzle pieces, that appears on our course materials. There are four puzzle pieces in the logo, each standing for one of the leadership action areas.

- *interpreting* conditions within and external to your organization that affect you and your work group (this is about assessing and being in touch with your environment)
- *shaping* vision and strategy to provide meaning for the work of the group (this is about involving people in the process)
- *mobilizing* individuals with different ideas, skills, and values to carry out the work of group (this is about getting it done)
- *inspiring* people to achieve results (this is about signing up your staff for the long term)

The twenty leadership practices are organized into four clusters of five, each cluster pertaining to one of the action areas listed here. The four puzzle pieces in the logo interlock to highlight the fact that the practices are all essential and interdependent. As the schedule shown in Exhibit 7.1 illustrates, over the next three days, we will cover each of the four clusters of leadership practices. We will also receive feedback on our current abilities relative to each cluster, based on preprogram surveys completed by our peers, subordinates, and superiors.

Before our individual feedback reports are given to us, we are put through the Margaret Lenton exercise, which serves as a conclusion to the introductory section of the program. We see a video of Margaret, a manager leading a cross-functional team in developing a new product called global checking. The exercise acquaints us better with the four leadership action areas and gives us the opportunity to evaluate a leader's use of the twenty practices.

We must evaluate Margaret's use of the twenty practices; these are the same twenty items that appear in our feedback reports, organized in the same manner. We form two small

Exhibit 7.1. Leadership Course Schedule.

	Day 1	Day 2	Day 3
Morning			
	Introduction Feedback	Shaping Mobilizing	Inspiring
Afternoon			
	Interpreting Shaping	Mobilizing	Inspiring Integration Closing

Source: The Forum Company. Copyright 1990. Reprinted with permission.

groups to discuss our ratings and agree on a score for Margaret in each of the four action areas. Diane asks each group to defend its ratings, and draws a bar graph on the flip chart to display our scores for Margaret.

We find that both groups are pretty much in agreement that Margaret is very weak on interpreting, not so strong on mobilizing, but definitely a winner when it comes to shaping and inspiring. Everyone agrees that Margaret is not very responsive to feedback. This brings up the question of performance evaluation: how do you get someone like that to improve his or her ways? All concur it could be difficult.

Feedback

Our final discussion of the Margaret Lenton exercise focuses on feedback and serves as a lead-in for us to receive and deal with our personal feedback reports. Three flip charts are produced:

1. Why feedback?
   - relevance to work
   - focus on specific actions
   - self-understanding
2. Report overview:
   - explanation
   - different elements
3. Look for:
   - your strengths
   - what you need to improve
   - what is most important in your situation
   - how your views compare with those of your associates

Once Diane has explained what we are about to receive, she cautions us as to the normal reactions to feedback, with which at least half the class seem to be very familiar: shock, anger, rejection, acceptance, help. Diane writes these on the central flip chart as we prepare to receive our reports.

In my situation—a student, not a manager—I find limited value in my feedback report. My scores tend to be high on all dimensions, which simply shows me that my friends think highly of me. Most of the other participants, however, spend considerable time going through their reports and seem to find the feedback instructive. Four of them eventually spend time with Diane outside the classroom in counseling sessions to understand their feedback in more depth. We each take a moment to record our reactions in journals provided in our course binders. The journals serve not only as diaries but as means to encourage deeper reflection. For each module in the course, the journal contains thought-provoking questions for us to answer.

Day 1, Afternoon: Interpreting

We start off with a little exercise. We divide into two groups, and my group, of four, moves into the room next door. Diane hands each of us five cards. On each card, there is a different statement (for example, "The manager with a staff of 150 sits to the right of the manager who knows which competitors are in which markets") as well as this instruction: "Although you may tell your group members what is printed on this slip of paper, you may not let anyone else read it." Diane then walks out of the room without giving any instructions.

As we look at our cards, it becomes apparent that two of them carry questions instead of statements: "Who knows about staff expansion in the company's MIS department?" and "Who should we talk to about trade in the Middle East?" The object of the exercise is to collate all our bits of information so as to answer these two questions.

I volunteer to go to the board and ask my fellow participants to read their statements, one by one. We figure out that the problem involves five individuals, and that we are provided with six categories of information on each one: (1) name; (2) who sits next to whom in the boardroom; (3) who is head of which department; (4) the number of staff each supervises; (5) a geographical area of expertise; (6) a functional area of expertise. Most of the statements only begin to make sense and yield usable information when they are combined with others.

I elect to use a matrix format, and we first figure out who

sits next to whom. We then fill in the blanks until the table is complete and we are capable of answering the questions. The two groups get back together again in the main classroom, and our two matrices are put up on the flip charts.

Diane asks us what helped the process. Everyone agrees that it was essential to write down the information; the other group actually started off by writing down all the statements. There was also general agreement on the need to set up a framework to understand the parameters of the exercise and to work as a team.

Most importantly, we are often stumped by assumptions we should not have been making: that the marketing person ought to be the one who knows about consumer preferences, for example. The moral of this, of course, is that we all make assumptions about ourselves and our environment, and that these assumptions can easily lead us astray. This directly influences how we interpret our context.

What also comes out of the process is that some of us have a greater tolerance than others for dealing with unstructured problems. In the other group, information was freely exchanged in a haphazard way until the right connections were finally made. One of the participants clearly did not enjoy the exercise; she needed structure and direction. In our group, the problem did not arise because information was collated much more efficiently.

We are then asked to make links between this exercise and our work situations. Mike, who was in the other group, noted that they proceeded without making any plans, "just mucking around," and that this was typical of how he often operated at work as well. Jocelyn, who was in my group, commented that in this case we really needed each other, knew it, and cooperated; in real life we need each other just as much but do not necessarily call on each other for help. (Fictitious names are used for all participants.) The principal lesson was that we should use many different sources of information to interpret our environment, and that we should be conscious and wary of assumptions.

Diane runs through the leadership traits in the interpreting cluster, which are as follows:[2]

Interpreting Practices

1. seeking information from as many sources as possible
2. knowing how your own work supports the organization's overall strategy
3. analyzing how well the members of the group work together
4. knowing the capabilities and motivations of the individuals in the work group
5. knowing your own capabilities and motivations

She concludes by explaining that leaders must master the interpretation skills in order to instill confidence and trust. A leader cannot afford to be out of touch.

We then turn to the booklet on interpreting and read the first few pages. A model is presented, illustrated by a bull's-eye that represents the four levels of interpretation: environment, organization, work group, and self. We are asked to list all the sources we can think of that can yield information at each level and are given fifteen minutes to fill out an interpretation matrix in the booklet. To conclude this segment, the following three key points on interpreting are written on the flip charts:

1. Interpret on four levels: environment, organization, work group, and self.
2. Identify patterns and select critical facts.
3. Set priorities for yourself and your work group.

We then move on to the next cluster of leadership practices, which involve shaping a vision.

Shaping

On the flip charts, we see the shaping objectives:

1. Understand what is required when you shape vision and strategy to provide meaning for the work of the group.
2. Describe your personal vision of leadership.
3. Shape a vision for the work group.

In addition, the shaping practices are written on the charts. (Of the four action areas, shaping is the second; the five practices for this area are numbered 6 through 10.)

Shaping Practices

6. involving the right people in developing the work group's strategy
7. standing up for what is important
8. adjusting plans and actions as necessary in turbulent situations
9. communicating the strategy of the organization as a whole
10. creating a positive picture of the future for the work group

Diane asks us to describe what happens when shaping is done well, and summarizes our comments on the flip charts. Among the statements she writes are these:

- Shaping builds excitement.
- Shaping builds a bridge that permits the group to make it through rough times.
- When shaping is done well, everyone sees the part they have to play.
- Everyone has a sense of mission.
- The need to micromanage disappears.

We turn to our personal feedback reports and examine our results on shaping. We are asked to single out our weakest shaping practice, so as to concentrate on it throughout the shaping exercises. Diane draws a model of the shaping process on the flip chart. Its purpose is to show that shaping occurs at four interdependent levels: organization, work group, task, and individual. Ideally, an individual's top ten values should be the organization's top ten as well; there should be a commonality of purpose.

The power and importance of shaping at the task level is stressed; if we concentrate on only one area after we leave here, this should be it. The idea behind shaping at the task level is to give direction on a day-to-day basis to motivate people, make them feel valuable, and give them a sense of mission.

Diane draws our attention to the weekly showcase board in Forum's lobby, on which all our names have been inscribed. The employee responsible for the lettering could simply have been told to do the job. Instead, she was made aware of how significant the job was: having his or her name up there makes the customer feel welcome and important, and Forum's mission is to serve its customers. Because she understands the importance of the task, the employee always double-checks each name's spelling; if the task had not been as well shaped as it was, Barry would have found his name written *Smithfeld* instead of *Smithfield*.

At the personal level, shaping involves figuring out one's values. The idea of a personal vision is to have a picture of yourself as a leader in the company and how you want to be viewed by others (customers, boss, peers, direct reports, and the like). It must also manifest the following characteristics of an ideal vision:

- clear
- involving
- relevant
- linked to overall strategy
- linked to customer needs
- memorable
- meaningful beyond work
- seen as a stretch (that is, not too easy to achieve)
- better than the current situation
- a reflection of group values

Frank describes his organization's vision, as expressed by its chairperson: each employee should not only think of but be *obsessed* with "customer delight." There is not one word on profit in the vision statement. Frank finds that this vision has tremendous stretch and attributes many recent quality innovations at his company to it. At a time when the company is going through dramatic cultural change, everyone, down to the lowest level, is expected to buy in. Some employees are apparently scared by the strength of the language used—especially the word *obsession*—which makes the customer the final arbiter of success. "Troop delight"—keeping the employees happy—is also very much emphasized.

Following the discussion, we fill out a worksheet on our personal visions. When Diane asks for volunteers to read out their visions, Sam is willing. He has come up with a vision statement for his work group, rather than for himself personally. It basically says that he wants their management development team to be the best team anywhere in the Western world.

Day 2, Morning: Shaping, Continued

Diane provides us with a recap of where we now stand. She reiterates that our group will not be working on organizational vision, which is included in the program when all participants are from the same company. Someone asks whether Diane finds that people are often surprised by how important interpreting is to effective leadership. She replies that people usually associate charisma and vision with leadership, but don't "zoom in" on interpreting as a key factor. Forum's research indicates that leadership primarily consists of a set of teachable skills, such as those pertaining to interpreting: "You don't have to be Joe Charisma to be a strong leader." Of the twenty practices Forum teaches, the one that correlates most highly with effective leadership is "promoting the development of people's talents."

To get back into shaping, we watch short video clips of people talking about their visions for their work teams. The ten elements of an ideal vision, introduced on day one, are put back up on the flip charts. We see three very short video segments, each approximately forty-five seconds in length, and after each one we rate the speaker with respect to the ten elements. Everybody participates freely and we get back into the topic.

Moving on, we take up the personal visions we have developed overnight. Frank agrees to share his vision with us; it is very close to the one Sam had devised the previous afternoon—that is, a group, as opposed to a personal, vision. Frank speaks of it being a "key compelling force" and providing the most exciting educational opportunities possible for employees. Frank says that he plans to distribute his vision statement to his customers to see what they think of it. Their responses will help him reshape it.

As we conclude the section on shaping, I realize that this part of the program would be more effective if all participants were from the same organization — it could help them integrate their personal values with their work-related goals.

Mobilizing

After a morning break, we come back to find the mobilizing objectives set out on the flip charts:

• to learn what is required to mobilize a work group
• to align its efforts with the larger organization
• to determine how values relate to mobilizing the group
• to apply mobilizing practices in leadership situations

The next five practices, those for the mobilizing action area (numbers 11 through 15), are also written on the flip charts.

Mobilizing Practices

11. communicating clearly the results expected from others
12. appealing to people's hearts and minds to lead them in a new direction
13. demonstrating care for the members of the work group
14. demonstrating confidence in the abilities of others
15. letting people know how they are progressing toward the group's goal

We review them and begin an exercise called Site-Central. Diane calls for three volunteers. Mary, Sam, and I raise our hands. Diane gives us an instruction sheet and ushers the other six participants into the room next door. We will be "Central" and they will be "Site."

We three read our instructions together and my first reaction, upon skimming the rules and the task description, is to run next door to see how Site is set up. What I find there is a grid laid out on the carpet with tape, and the six participants standing on it facing each other in a particular order. Our group is assigned to reorder them, following the rules, so that they end up standing in a very different order.

I ask no questions, but simply survey the situation and run back to Central to show Sam and Mary what we have to do. After experimenting with the problem on paper for a few minutes, I go get props: three juice glasses and three coffee cups. Mary writes identifying letters on them and within minutes we have figured out the principle. I run back to Site and order the people in that group to move until they are all standing where they should. I then turn to Diane and declare that the task is done. She asks me if I am sure, and I say yes. I rejoin my group at Central, and Diane gives us discussion questions to work on before the entire group is brought back together again. The problem-solving exercise, for which forty minutes had been allotted, took just under ten minutes, from start to finish.

It is only after we begin reading the discussion questions that I figure out that we have missed the whole point of the exercise — mobilizing Site. The thought of calling on Site members to help solve the problem never occurred to me. In my problem-solving mode, I become completely task driven; the fact that the people standing on the Site grid were anything more than the cups we were playing with in the other room was irrelevant to me.

After a few minutes, the Site people come back in. They tell us that they felt used, bored (standing on a grid for ten minutes can seem very long indeed), and angry. They had been given only one instruction: that they should do nothing without the explicit instructions or approval of Central personnel — therefore they never knew what the exercise was all about. Frank comments that my first visit "felt like a typical corporate visit — they just don't care." When I explain how we arrived at the solution, Mike exclaims, "Well, we felt like cups." Diane, to some extent, comes to my rescue, saying that none of the Site members exhibited any leadership—no one asked me any questions during my visits.

Jocelyn comments that this exercise provides another example of how assumptions can get in the way: I had obviously assumed that Site knew what the game was all about. I also had assumed that I was racing against the clock; I always put myself in "fast forward" when there is a problem to be solved. Frank asks why the problem had been given to Central and not to Site; after all, it was a Site problem and Central should not have been the ones solving it. He further comments that this was quite typical of the way things happen in the corporate world. In many ways, then, this exercise nicely captures the realities of organizations.

As to the way I essentially took over the show—Sam and Mary just watched me—Diane simply comments that there will be times when I cannot solve the problem on my own, so I'd better get in the habit of asking for help and working as a team player. The point is well taken. I felt quite embarrassed at the end of the exercise because it showed so accurately how I operate. I realize my solo performance can be alienating to others, and this exercise provided considerable insight to me.

To conclude the exercise, we take another look at the five mobilizing practices in the context of what has just occurred. We all agree that "communicating clearly the results expected from others" is the most important. We then turn to our journal to record our thoughts on the Site-Central exercise. Once done, we adjourn for lunch.

Day 2, Afternoon: Mobilizing, Continued

After lunch, we continue with the mobilizing segment. Diane divides us into two teams for the mobilizing lab, which will take up the whole afternoon. Sam, Nancy, Jocelyn, and Frank are Team 1. Ann, Lily, Mike, Mary, and Barry are Team 2.

The purpose of the lab is written on the flip chart: "to apply leadership practices for mobilizing in a work situation." We are Blazetech Industries, involved in the manufacture of aircrafts. We begin with an address by our company CEO on video. Our team then moves to the room next door, where supplies have been set up for us.

The exercise is divided into four parts, and we have to elect a different leader for each section. We decide to draw lots, with the following results: Lily will chair Part 1, Barry will chair Part 2, Mary will chair Part 3, and Ann will chair Part 4.

Each leader has to decide beforehand which of the five mobilizing practices he or she wants to concentrate on while at the helm. I opt for "communicating clearly the results expected from others," since its importance was driven home that morning; Barry chooses it as well. Lily says she will take "demonstrate confidence in the abilities of others," and Mary takes "appeal to people's hearts and minds to lead them in a new direction." At the end of each section, we are to give our feedback reports to the leader, paying special attention to whether the chosen practice was mastered.

Lily is our first leader. We turn to our booklet on mobilizing, which includes the instructions for our exercise. It lists the planning activities we need to do before we begin the exercise and gives us information on the company's background as well as a speech by Blazetech's CEO, which contains his philosophy and values. Lily reads the introduction aloud and continues to read until she reaches the instruction "list in the left-hand column the values that motivate our chairman." She then becomes silent and waits for us to do it. We have to distill the CEO's important values from the speech. I say nothing; after this morning, I am resolved to play a secondary role until it is my turn to lead. Mary says nothing. Barry says nothing. Lily says nothing. Finally, Mike kicks it off by suggesting that perseverance is important to our chairman. I add that innovation is, as well. We finally put together a list. Then we must decide whether the chairman's beliefs are consistent with our own. All of them are consistent with mine, but the other three participants cannot accept "hard work." We settle on saying that it is consistent with our beliefs, but only "within limits."

We continue Part 1, with Lily's contribution as leader consisting strictly of reading the text and reminding us periodically of how much time we have left to complete this section. I try very hard not to take over, but Barry and Lily insist on keeping quiet. Mike and I end up answering all the questions; I try to get the others to voice their opinions, but I feel very self-conscious because that ought to be the leader's job — and I'm not the leader. The process is uncomfortable. We finally fill out the feedback worksheets for Lily, keeping in mind that she was apparently trying to "demonstrate confidence in the abilities of others."

We begin Part 2 of the exercise — developing a paper airplane prototype for manufacturing — and now it is Barry's turn. He begins by reading the instructions from the booklet for producing the paper airplane prototype. As he reads, I realize that our objective is to maximize profit. When he finishes, Barry assigns different people to different prototypes. I remind him, as meekly as possible, that it simply might not be profitable to make certain models, and that before jumping into prototype production we should first consider the product information to determine the optimal production plan. Barry does not give up on his notion of immediate production, so I do not insist; I simply volunteer to take charge of the numbers. I quickly determine that we should concentrate on a model called Stork Wing airplane, which yields the highest profit per minute of production. We are told that we have a maximum contract quota of sixty-five of these, but that is a number we cannot reach, given the production time allotted. I also figure that if we all concentrate on a single model, we will be more efficient; learning curve effects might start happening. I communicate my findings to Barry, who agrees; however, he does not halt the production of the other prototypes.

Meanwhile, Sam, who is with the other group, comes in to see how we are doing. Sam and I both learned a lesson this morning and decide that consultation and cooperation ought to be our watchwords from now on. I show him my profit numbers, and we decide that if our two teams were to merge production capacities we could realize a huge profit and make our CEO really happy. We decide that we should build sixty-five Stork Wings and throw in a Carousel airplane or two if we have the time. Barry is too busy supervising prototype production to realize that a merger has just happened.

We face a problem: time is running out and Mike cannot figure out from the model drawings how to build the Stork Wing. Unless we have a prototype that meets specifications, we cannot build. Barry tells him, "I know you can do it," but that does not help. Lily runs to Mike's rescue, but Mike is increasingly frustrated and refuses her help. I decide that we need a Stork Wing, and I build one. I show Mike how the folds are made and hand him my prototype to fly. Mike flies it, and it meets specs. However, Mike is still upset because he could not build it himself and has serious reservations about committing to an all–Stork Wing production plan. I tell him that there is only one fold that he did not get, that we will all build one together — it is not that difficult, and we can all get the hang of it.

Meanwhile the other group's Stork Wing does not meet specifications, and the plan to merge dissolves. In any event, Diane informs us that we are supposed to be working independently this time. (You never know with these exercises — you either cooperate too much or too little!)

We now have to fill out feedback reports on Barry. The task is not an easy one — Barry had elected to "communicate clearly the results expected from others," but, in fact, he communicated very little if at all.

Time for Part 3, producing the aircraft. Mary takes over as leader. She doesn't say a word but starts building a Stork Wing in the corner, on her own. I see Barry, Mike, and Lily through the production of their first plan, and they get the hang of it. Mary comes to me when she is near completion because she needs help with one of the final steps. We all get heavily involved in Stork Wing production. We have half an hour to build as many as we can, and our little factory is happily buzzing away, in a blissful, leaderless fashion.

Fifteen minutes into production, Diane gives us an urgent memo from our CEO. Mary reads it quietly in her corner, but we are too busy building to pay much attention. Finally she tells us that there is a malfunction in the directional equipment and that we have to make a decision. She gives no further details and none of us is sure what we should do. I ask her for additional directions, but it still is not clear. I ask Mary if I can see the memo; I would rather not take this initiative, since it means I am again taking the lead, but I feel I have to. I get the others' attention: we have to decide to stop production because of the malfunction and incur a penalty for late delivery, or take some other action. Lily and Barry keep working, but Mike and I arrive at a decision: we should continue building, immediately advise the client of the problem, and find another supplier for directional equipment. Mary writes this down and hands it back to Diane. We incur a $100,000 penalty for having spent too much time answering the memo.

Production time runs out, and we end up with twenty-four Stork Wings in the Blazetech hangar. Half of them have malfunctioning directional equipment, but Mike, our official pilot, flies all of them in the hallway anyway. All but three perform to specifications. Since each good plane brings us a $100,000 profit, we end up with $2 million in the bank ($2,100,000 minus the $100,000 penalty). We complete the production report, and Mary's tenure is officially over; we just have to fill out her feedback reports.

It is now officially my turn to lead, as we summarize the group's work. This is essentially a group self-assessment. I feel uncomfortable; I fear that I have ended up running the show again, even if I was not supposed to, and even if I was consciously trying not to. I am afraid the others must resent me. I try to be low-key as we complete our group assessment. I let the others arrive at the ratings about the group; my feeling about it, which I do not share with the others, is that the group was in fact not led at all, except to the extent that I was ready to give it direction. I am not happy about the way the participants worked together, and I would have rated us low on all the practices.

We agree that production became our consuming passion. We all lost track of the values we had written down at the start. I make the comment that norms and values emerge out of group dynamics; you cannot simply set them in advance. Similarly, you cannot impose a leader on a group. The others seem to agree.

We have to make a presentation of the lessons we learned, the values and practices that guided our work, and our production results to Diane and the other group. I ask if anyone wants to deliver it. They all tell me I should do it, so I agree to.

The two groups get back together again in the main classroom. Sam's group starts the presentations. They are all glowing—obviously they had a great time, and I know by looking at their faces that the process worked better for them than it did for us. They all participate, each presenting the section he or she led. It is clear that they were successful in rotating the leadership; that the nominal leader did take charge, and that the others followed his or her direction. They say they listened to each other, and that the group changed dramatically in orientation from phase to phase. Frank instituted a bonus system during the production phase, which kept them all happy and motivated (and which Diane outlawed). They kept track of their initial standards, particularly regarding safety; they checked every plane twice. The urgent memo completely stopped the group, and they resumed production only when the entire team had agreed on a solution. Their group worked the way I feel ours should have. They ended up with a final profit of $1 million.

It is now my turn to make our presentation. I start off by saying that I would like the others in my group to pitch in with any additional comments they might have. I say that we focused from the start on profit maximization, and that we ended with a final figure of $2 million. I then add, although I feel unsure of myself, that the leadership rotation did not work well in our group, and that we did not stick to the values we first set out for ourselves. I make my comments about norms, values, and leaders emerging out of group dynamics and being hard to impose. I also say that we all got into a sort of leaderless production frenzy.

Jocelyn comments that while our team made more money, she thinks her team would have sustained higher profit levels over time. Frank compares the two teams to General Motors and Honda (I suspect he sees us as GM).

We are asked what made the difference between the two teams. Jocelyn and Sam suggest that individual differences are the main factor, and I agree. Jocelyn adds that she is typically very production driven, and that she probably would have fit right in with our group. Diane comments that our group was functioning like a well-oiled machine during the production process. Because we didn't have an effective leader, we would have had a hard time dealing with change or turbulence. A group like ours could only work in a stable environment.

Sam, Frank, Jocelyn, and I decide to have dinner together that evening. They spend some time giving me pointers on how to manage people; this was probably the most valuable part of the program for me.

Day 3, Morning: Inspiring

Diane begins the morning by asking us why inspiring is so important. Our answers, which she writes on the chart, are it gets people to do more than they think they can, and it permits execution.

Diane then turns to one of the other flip charts, on which the objectives of the module on inspiring are listed:

- to analyze how leaders inspire people
- to understand that inspiration is critical to achieving and sustaining successful efforts
- to apply inspiring practices to your work situation

She emphasizes that inspiring and charisma are not the same thing. The essence of inspiring is in how others react; it is giving others the leadership role. You have to think of inspiration from the point of view of the person being inspired. We review our personal feedback reports on inspiring and identify any weak areas we might want to work on.

Half of the class is then asked to think about situations in which their commitment declined because of bad leadership; the other half is asked to think about situations in which, on the contrary, they were inspired to do their best. We are given five minutes to think of examples, which we then share with the others. Diane writes the highlights on the chart. The examples of bad leadership share the following characteristics:

- leader not interested
- didn't do what he or she committed to
- didn't learn from him or her

- didn't get others involved
- didn't communicate clearly

We now turn to examples of good leadership. Again, the characteristics that stand out are written on the board:

- boss thought employee could do the job
- employee felt inspired by boss's confidence
- boss knew how to ask questions in ways that made the employee feel safe
- boss challenged employee and could accept failure
- boss exhibited high energy
- boss empowered and provided support for employee

Diane now exhibits the five inspiring practices:

Inspiring Practices

16. promoting the development of people's talents
17. recognizing the contributions of others
18. enabling others to feel and act like leaders
19. stimulating others' thinking
20. building enthusiasm about projects and assignments

With respect to "promoting the development of people's talents," she repeats that of the twenty practices espoused by Forum, this was the once most closely correlated with good leadership. As to the next practice, "recognizing the contributions of others," she states, "It doesn't matter if you have confidence in someone if they don't know it."

We go on to a case study: Jim Van Zoren, parts A, B and C. Diane leads us in a lively classroom debate of the cases. The purpose of the exercise is to show us the importance and the interrelatedness of the twenty leadership practices.

After the morning break, we participate in a "hotline" exercise, which will be tied back into the inspiring practices. The idea is to have us call on our group members (as we would on a hotline) for help with a current job situation. The situation, however, is very specific: it must require inspiring others to do something that is very important yet difficult. Suggestions can be what we have learned from the inspiring practices or from our own knowledge and experience. The central question each participant must answer in the exercise is, "How have I tried to inspire others in this situation?" We spend five minutes filling out worksheets beforehand; we then meet in small groups and discuss our problems. I am assigned to Jocelyn and Mike.

Jocelyn and I know each other fairly well after our dinner together the previous evening, and we have already spent a few hours going over our respective leadership problems and work frustrations. I therefore try to get Mike, whom I plan to handle gently because of the Stork Wing affair, to air his problems first. His feedback report shows that he is very weak at inspiring, and particularly at "building enthusiasm about projects and assignments." He explains that he has been designing training programs for sales teams for fifteen years, and that he finds it difficult to get excited. As he puts it, "When you've peeled a hundred potatoes, you know what the hundred-and-first is going to look like even before you start peeling it." Jocelyn and I try to make helpful suggestions; for one thing, he might do well to stop thinking of his job in terms of potatoes that need to be peeled, and instead try to get in touch with his subordinates' feelings.

Jocelyn's problem is that she does not like her current boss; in fact, she is working on a transfer. They both turn to me. My problem is that I am the de facto leader of my MBA business policy course group, the project is due next Monday, and the others have yet to put any work into it. What should I do? Part of my quandary is that I have very high standards, I am not sure any of my colleagues can live with them, and I do not have time to find out. Jocelyn and Mike give me good advice about participative management, which I think about for the next few hours. Once the exercise is over we break for lunch.

Day 3, Afternoon: Inspiring, Continued

Back from lunch, we prepare to give "inspiring talks." The flip chart reads:

1. Think of a work situation that is really important. Consider:
    *   your vision
    *   hot-line work
    Imagine that you are meeting with people involved. What would you say?
2. Plan a three-minute talk. Consider:
    *   inspiring practices
    *   group values
    *   images and phrases that draw on emotions
3. Then, in small groups:
    *   give your talks
    *   use inspiration index
    *   give and get advice on how to inspire

We are given fifteen minutes to prepare our talks. We get back into our small groups — the same ones as this morning — and give our talks. Diane concludes this section by reminding us once again that inspiring and charisma are not the same thing. The key points to remember are written on the flip chart:

1. Inspire with actions.
2. Create leaders, not followers.
3. Share the work and the success.

Frank adds a fourth: "Know your audience." Mike comments that you cannot master the five inspiring practices unless you have already mastered the other fifteen.

Integrating

In the final hour of the program, we integrate the four clusters of leadership behaviors. We are shown a video of adults talking about leadership. We are then given fifteen minutes to fill out a planning worksheet in our journal. This is meant to help us transfer what we have learned during the past three days back to our work situations.

Finally, we divide into two groups for the closing exercise: we are asked to illustrate what leadership now means to us "through pictures, symbols, music, poetry, skills, stories, dance, or any other socially acceptable behavior."

I find myself in the room next door with Lily, Mike, and Barry—my Stork Wing group from yesterday. We sit down and start asking ourselves what leadership means to us. Lily volunteers to go to the board to write down our thoughts. We write down some statements, such as "leaders listen." I make the comment that a notable aspect of the week was the Stork Wing exercise. The others agree that that was the highlight—so we decide to build a giant Stork Wing with flip chart paper and decorate it with all our thoughts on leadership. I am put in charge of production, and we decorate our plane like a World War II Japanese bomber. As we each write down our favorite leadership statement on the wings, Barry notices that all four of us are left-handed, and comments that left-handedness is particularly prevalent among great leaders. We all feel good about that.

The two groups get back together. Mike flies our Stork Wing bomber through the main classroom, and the other group does a song-and-dance skit. We all thank Diane and call it a day.

Part Three

Lessons for Leadership Training

Chapter Eight

Art, Science, or Fad?
A Critique of
Leadership Programs

*T*here are many paths to enlightenment.
— Anonymous New Age Philosopher

Our experiences in the five programs we participated in taught us that while each one could be helpful, there was no one best program for leadership training. Each had distinct strengths and drawbacks. Our purpose in this chapter is to step back from the details of our experiences and attempt to answer the important question, What kinds of developmental outcomes might we expect from each approach? We will begin with the personal growth programs.

The Personal Growth Approaches

As we have noted before, the personal growth programs have attracted the greatest interest and the greatest notoriety. Unlike traditional skills-based or conceptual programs, personal growth approaches offer the novelty of psychological interventions and exercises. Because much of the work is done on an emotional level, participants often report dramatic or, at the least, very memorable experiences.

Most of the personal growth approaches rest on two simple premises. First, many of us have lost touch with our innermost values, talents, passions, and sense of power because of societal and work-life expectations. Through personal growth experiences, we can reconnect with these inner qualities and allow them to emerge in our work and personal life. Second, our fears of failing or of rejection are the major reason we are out of touch with our inner potential. By addressing these, we can move beyond them and experiment with developing ourselves.

The link that these programs make to leadership is the following: leaders are individuals who are deeply in touch with their gifts and passions. Therefore, only by tapping into and realizing one's passions can a person become a leader. Thus, if training can help managers get in touch with their talents and sense of purpose, they will presumably have the motivation and enthusiasm to formulate inspiring visions and to motivate those who work for them.

In addition, since most of these programs have grown out of the human potential movement of the 1960s and 1970s, they often make the additional assumption that only a "whole" person can become an effective leader. By "whole," they mean an individual whose personal and work life are in balance and whose emotions are clear and accessible. In this view, interpersonal problems are the results of an unbalanced life and emotional state and will block an individual's ability to be an effective leader. Soon we will see whether these assumptions are realistic. But first, we begin with a bit of history.

History of the Personal Growth Programs

As mentioned in earlier chapters, the groundwork for programs focusing on personal growth was laid as far back as the 1960s, when the National Training Laboratories in Bethel, Maine, initiated T-groups. Managers attended week-long intensive sessions to learn how their behavior affected others and how to accept feedback from others. Often assisted by psychologist facilitators, participants in small working groups would share with each other the positive and negative consequences of their behavior. This process operated on the assumption that the first step in being a good manager was knowing yourself—your strengths and limitations. It also assumed that if people could see the negative impact of certain of their behaviors they could correct these and in turn become more effective managers. Personal growth as interpreted by these programs was the ability to be interpersonally competent and emotionally open. These values continued to permeate leadership training into the 1980s.

Developing in parallel during the 1970s were the human potential and New Age movements. Humanistic psychotherapies such as Gestalt and Transactional Analysis had popularized therapy as a personal growth activity for the "normal" individual, and the search for self-fulfillment beginning in the 1960s had increased the popularity and acceptability of psychotherapy. Soon "mass therapeutic experiences" were being introduced through public seminars. A controversial figure, Werner Erhard, emerged during this time with his est (Erhard Seminar Training) program. Centered around a sixty-hour marathon training experience, the program was conducted over two weekends and combined elements of a conventional encounter group with the rigors of a Marine Corps boot camp. The experience promised participants greater creativity, energy, and vitality, and better relationships. Most of the teachings for these programs came from the humanistic psychologies. As well, Eastern religions, especially Buddhism, had an impact, with their emphasis on understanding how the emotions push and pull at the human mind, interfering with its ability to focus. By the late 1970s and early 1980s, the est programs became so popular that some half a million Americans attended them at an average price of $360 per person. Soon afterward, similar programs appeared, such as Lifespring.

A central premise of est and of other personal growth programs has been that individuals need to take responsibility for their own lives. Est, for example, has operated on the assumption that most of us allow the responsibility for our lives to lie outside of our control. As a result, we feel powerless and unhappy. Est continually reminds participants to be in control of their destinies, to stop blaming others for their sense of power-lessness. Given a growing sense of alienation and powerlessness in society during the 1970s, the idea that one could control one's own destiny naturally had great appeal.

In addition, Maslow's concept of self-actualization was heavily promoted. For example, est and other programs have emphasized that human beings need to fulfill the potential of their personal gifts while contributing to the greater good of so-ciety. Drawing from the humanistic psychologies, seminar lead-ers told their participants that self-actualization was achievable through their own powers. The problem, they argued, was that most people were waiting for outside resources, such as more money or a better job or a better education, to change our situ-ation, but, est argued (as does Buddhism), these were only il-lusions. Self-actualization could result simply from a change of heart and mind manifested in the present moment. The "here-and-now" moment, therefore, has been a central focus of these programs. They have argued that too many people live for tomorrow, with a false hope of what it would bring them, rather than living in the present moment and actively taking respon-sibility for what they have created for themselves.

For est and its management seminar counterpart, the Forum, enlightenment has meant living life in the "presence" (a play on the word *present*) rather than in "concept" (ideas and fantasies about life). "To live in the presence" means being max-imally aware, open, trusting, and committed in this moment. "To live in concepts" means being preoccupied with dreams, hopes, fears, and narrow theories of one's world. By "living in the presence" a person presumably becomes aware of all of his or her internal resources and strengths and, in turn, of all pos-sibilities and options. These newly sensed options, as well as the individual's enlightened ability to see and act, open up the potential for more creative contributions — and in management settings, for more effective leadership.

These key ideas (take responsibility, live in the present, realize your potential) have permeated most of the personal growth programs involving leadership training. For example, it is not surprising that we hear Larry Wilson of the Pecos River program saying, "Changing the game is the strategy we are working on here at the ranch [Pecos River]. Changing the game is another way of taking charge of your life, of being in control of yourself instead of being the victim, while everything around you is unpredictable. It's a way of being responsible and accountable, but at the same time knowing that you don't run the universe. . . . John Crystal said that the start of every person's development is to find their unique talents and let that become how they start and how they grow."[1]

A third profound influence on the personal growth programs was the outdoor-adventure organization Outward Bound. Throughout the 1960s and 1970s, their programs proliferated to meet the demands of the then-teenage baby boomers for an outdoor rite-of-passage experiences. By the 1970s, this market had essentially stopped growing; the teenagers had become adults. In response, Outward Bound turned its sights to adults and businesses. Wilderness adventures were marketed to the corporate world as a means of building teams and encouraging greater leadership back at the office. These outdoor programs influenced the personal growth programs of the 1980s, with their notions of risk taking and teamwork. If managers could successfully rappel down cliffs and raft difficult river rapids, then they could surely exhibit greater boldness and risk taking on the job. If managers could successfully bond together in teams to make decisions while hiking in uncharted areas, then they could surely exhibit greater teamwork back on the job.

While both assumptions appeared attractive, they were not necessarily accurate. The workplace was in many ways a radically different environment from the wilderness. And real workplace teams had a tendency to rapidly gain and lose their members as teammates moved on to new jobs or left for other opportunities. This mobility common to corporations often negated all the team-building efforts that had gone on in the wilderness experience. In addition, the prior conditioning of the workplace environment was often so strong that returning teams would revert immediately back to their old noncollaborative ways. As one executive explained to me, "You can take the wild beasts out of the jungle and tame them, but once you put them back, they become wild beasts again."

A fourth influence on the orientation of the personal

growth programs was the Peace Corps. John F. Kennedy had sent many young people abroad in the 1960s to help in the Third World. These young men and women returned to the United States with the desire to continue making a positive contribution, and a number of them ended up in training or training-related functions. Their values around human growth would permeate the programs they designed. A striking example of this is the Center for Creative Leadership, where several key program designers are graduates of the Peace Corps. As well, one of the founders of The Leadership Challenge program, Jim Kouzes, is a Peace Corps graduate. These former Peace Corps members brought to leadership training the ideas of contributing to the well-being of others (employees and customers) and affirming the goal of self-actualization.

These four orientations—National Training Laboratories, the humanistic psychology movement, Outward Bound, and the Peace Corps—were the primary forces behind the personal growth programs that emerged in the 1980s. They brought a distinct humanistic concern to training. Leaders were perceived as individuals who were concerned about others' growth as well as their own; they sought higher meaning in the workplace, they were risk takers, they valued teamwork, they placed a premium on trust and openness, they believed in taking responsibility for one's life. Programs sought to teach these values and to demonstrate their effectiveness in the workplace. To a great extent, these values were appealing, yet they were idealistic. The question remained whether such beliefs and values could help managers transform themselves into leaders.

A Closer Look at the Assumptions

When looking at the personal growth programs, an important question to ask is whether the premises and goals, attractive as they may seem, are realistic and accurate. Let us start with the idea of taking responsibility for one's life. Essentially, the aim of these programs is to empower—to help participants see the extent to which they have forsaken their own sense of power or efficacy in the workplace and in their personal lives. They achieve this awareness in participants through either outdoor adventures that involve risk taking and a sense of personal mastery or through indoor experiential exercises that force participants to reflect on the discrepancy between what they want in their lives and their present reality. These experiences, in the end, allow participants a taste of their personal power. Ultimately, they are designed to jar participants into seeing how much of their own power they have relinquished. As a result, they can be eye-opening, if they are carried out properly.

The problem for participants is that they must return back to the workplace. So, for example, while managers participating in these programs report becoming more open to taking personal risks, many found this behavior difficult to implement at work because of the conservatism of their organizations. Instead, we discovered that participants' newfound sense of risk taking more often manifested itself in their private lives, in terms of extracurricular activities such as scuba diving or sharing more personally with their families.

We know from the work of psychologist B. F. Skinner that only if a behavior is reinforced is it likely to be instilled. Avoiding, rather than taking, risks is more often rewarded by organizations, so conservatism is reinforced on the participant's return to the office. There are, however, behaviors involving taking responsibility that are desired and rewarded by organizations. For example, I learned from subordinate feedback in one program that I was not always keeping my secretary informed of my schedule. Upon returning from the program, I changed this behavior. In this situation, both she and the organization valued this behavior and therefore encouraged or reinforced it. As a result, I am supported in my attempts to change this particular behavior. Organizations would have to actively identify areas of risk taking they wished to encourage and then reward managers in these areas.

So when participants describe a change in their ability to "take responsibility," it often has to do with what are seen as positive behaviors or incremental changes that are not challenging to their organizations' status quo. For example, the following is a representative comment: "I am much more likely to do advance preparation for work and to consider things in detail than I was before the course. I am also less opinionated and more participative with my employees. On performance appraisals, I will let my staff express their opinions and say how they want to develop rather than how I want them to develop. The change has been particularly strong back at home. I have changed how I deal with my two teenagers. I now make a conscious effort to be less directive, to listen to them, and to give more consideration to their ideas and points of view."

Yet for most of the personal growth programs the idea of taking responsibility is not so much directed at being prompt with paperwork or delegating (work-related tasks) as it is oriented toward the ideals of self-actualization and self-acceptance. In other words, it involves getting in touch with your personal talents, gifts, and interests. Once done, the theory goes, the likelihood of becoming a leader increases because, as the designers of these programs argue, leaders are deeply in touch with their skills and what excites them. And from the perspective of what we know about leadership, it does appear that leaders are indeed people who are passionate about their ideas and who do seem to be in touch with their talents and gifts.

The personal growth programs assume that most of us have buried within us a similar passion for something. This assumption, however, may simply not be true and may explain why we found few participants "getting in touch" with their passions. Young managers, for instance, may not have enough experience to know what their talents and interests are. Furthermore, simply getting in touch with these talents is no guarantee of leadership (and, admittedly, no program argues this explicitly). In many cases, an individual's talents may be unrelated to leading. For example, a manager's real talent might be in engineering or research or, a more extreme example, a talent to be an actress or a musician. In simple terms, many passions have nothing to do with leadership.

To counter this difficulty, many of these programs argue that by supporting individuals' realization of their more deeply held interests they provide a process not only to promote leaders but to weed out nonleaders. Those who discover a love of the theater or for running an antique store may simply choose to leave their organizations, thanks to the seminar. It is assumed that those who remain at their workplace are therefore more committed and more passionate about their work and about leading. Again, this is not necessarily so. Those who remain, even after discovering their passion for something else, may choose to stay on the job because they perceive the necessary resources or risks involved in leaving to be too significant. Others may not be resourceful enough to leave or they may be very security conscious.

Another premise of personal growth programs is that the process of getting participants in touch with their deeper values will translate into greater leadership ability and ultimately more humanistic leadership. Because of their human potential orientation, personal growth programs focus heavily on values around caring for others and emotional happiness. They attempt to help participants connect with these values within them. Yet, again, there is no necessary connection between humanistic values and leadership. Some good leaders are known to be autocratic.

But an outcome of this humanistic orientation was that participants reported improvements in their personal life. Getting in touch with values around caring, for example, allowed individuals to see what trade-offs they had made in their family life. Not so paradoxically, as programs promote such values, concerns turn to private life, not usually to work life. The family allows us to live out our deeper emotional needs, such as giving and receiving love, which the workplace cannot hope to fulfill or promote. So getting in touch with one's values around loving and sensitivity does not necessarily translate into becoming an effective leader at the office.

Another faulty premise of the personal growth programs is that leaders are whole, balanced individuals, that they have learned to lead harmonious lives, both in their work and personal spheres. Therefore the programs address the shortcomings in participants' personal lives as well as in their work lives. This belief reflects the influence of the humanistic therapies, which encouraged people to seek balance in their personal lives. In addition, competencies in personal intimacy or self-disclosure are assumed to be critical to leadership effectiveness — another influence of the humanistic psychology movement.

Anyone who has studied leaders knows that these two assumptions are incorrect. Many leaders do not have a balanced personal and work life. The vast majority are consumed by their work. It is a passion. Some might argue that to become a truly great leader, one must sacrifice the personal or family side. There are only so many hours in a day, and the visions and goals of effective leaders are so demanding and all-consuming that few individuals find the time for a balanced life. Also, many, though not all, leaders have a difficult time expressing personal feelings. The ability to disclose deeply held emotions is not a common characteristic. Some psychologists even argue that the inability to be in touch with unconscious emotional quandaries is what propels individuals to become leaders in the first place.

I am aware of one individual, for example, who up to his midlife years had been an active and highly respected leader. After a year of psychotherapy, he discovered that much of his desire to lead was tied to an unconscious craving for his father's attention (which he had not received as a child). As a child, he strove to get his father's attention through leading others and getting their respect (and then, ultimately, his father's respect). The adult in him had forgotten this unconscious struggle. Upon discovering the roots of his need, he shifted to pursuits other than leadership. He did, however, end up with a more balanced life. In conclusion, the personal growth programs present an ideal — the whole person — that may be contradicted by the reality of most leaders, despite what we would like to think.

From the perspective of training leaders, there are other premises that may be faulty. Personal growth approaches make the assumption that fears are our major stumbling blocks to greater creativity and risk taking, the latter being two somewhat common hallmarks of leadership. In large part, they may be correct. What can be challenged, however, is the assumption that the experience or metaphor of risk taking in a training environment context is easily transferable to a work environment. For example, is the mind-set required to jump off a cliff in New Mexico one that I can use back in my office as I contemplate making a risky investment in a new product? Will that experience carry over? And just as importantly, will it carry over in a constructive way, so that I do not take reckless chances with my organization's resources?

The answer to the first question is that we do not know. Numerous participants report being more self-confident than before, but they also say, as noted earlier, that their organizations' expectations that they would be risk-averse still prevented most of them from having the confidence to take risks. As far as the question of transfer is concerned, cliff-jumping does not provide a set of guidelines or rules that will apply to appraising risk in other situations. That part of the risk equation — a realistic assessment — it cannot provide. It might, however, effect a positive shift in mind-set so that individuals become more open to risk altogether. Given that organizations typically err on the side of conservatism rather than an openness to risk, reinforcing self-confidence toward constructive risk taking is in itself potentially very positive.

In addition, while most participants report an initial high during the first few weeks after completing one of these programs, within approximately three months, they say, the realities of everyday life supplant the thrills of cliff-jumping. Few described becoming a more successful leader as a result of their experiences. Those who attended with intact work groups did, however, describe the experience as solidifying the bonds of team members and promoting a level of openness not experienced before. A personal vision exercise did lead several people to find new jobs, to redefine their jobs, to perform charitable work, or to spend more time with their families. Few, however, said that outsiders would notice any long-term change.

Given this lengthy critique of the personal growth approaches, what value can these programs hope to offer us in terms of leadership development? Realistically, they offer opportunities for managers to experience teamwork, risk taking, emotional expressiveness, self-acceptance, and reflection, and they may in some cases offer a permanent change in behavior.

Our research revealed that participants took away from these experiences what was most salient for them at their particular stage or moment in life. People, in essence, latch on to events or ideas that help them grow personally with issues that they are now facing. For example, when I attended the Pecos River program, I had just received tenure at my university. I was struggling with the fact that I now had lifetime job security and had overcome what in my occupation was considered to be the most difficult career hurdle. I found myself asking, Is this all there is to life? I now had more security than I could imagine. Risk taking became an important issue once I was surrounded with security. In the Pecos River program, my most vivid experiences had to do with outdoor adventures involving risk. They became a metaphor for me when I returned to the university. At work, I began to undertake a series of risky, innovative curriculum changes in my courses.

Another participant in the Pecos River program was experiencing a midlife crisis centered around her having traded personal intimacy for career success. For her, the most vivid experiences were the exercises involving personal vulnerability and intimacy with others. So each participant takes what he or she needs from such programs, given their particular stage in life.

Interestingly, it is often a single idea, value, concept, or experience that participants say they have incorporated into their lives and used to make choices. Eventually, this single element becomes so much a part of their value or belief system that they take for granted its association with a particular program. In addition, certain outdoor adventures or personal growth exercises can jar participants into another view of themselves. For example, during the VisionQuest (ARC) program, I had an emotionally powerful insight during one of the personal growth exercises. To this day, I remember it vividly and still use it as a guide in making certain decisions. It jarred my view of myself and ultimately helped me redefine a part of myself.

Since many of the experiences of the personal growth programs occur on an emotional level, they appear to have a more lasting impact on participants than, say, the behavioral skill training or conceptual knowledge programs. For example, participants in the Pecos River program often described the outdoor adventures as challenging them on an emotional level.

Surprisingly, they were able to draw connections between the adventure experiences and their everyday lives. A representative comment would be, "The ropes course was unforgettable. This was by far the greatest learning experience. I really saw for the first time the split between the gut and the head. My heart was not buying what my mind was telling me — and that was that everything was okay. It's something that more businesses should pay attention to because I see a lot of people acting one way but feeling another. I guess it also taught me a lot about the mythical dragon (fear of failing) within. I often ask myself now what kind of dragon lies between myself and what I want. Now I ask myself, Okay, what's my worst fear here? What's the worst that can happen? Am I going to die? No. So now I can see my fears more clearly and then decide what to do."

A particular VisionQuest exercise (which I describe in detail in Chapter Four) forced me to come to grips with my own reality on an emotional level. It is on the level of emotions that I believe our greatest learning can often take place and lead to behavioral change. We do know from research that the more levels of an individual — emotional, imaginative, cognitive, and behavioral — are engaged by a learning experience, the more powerful the learning will be. This is the distinct advantage of the personal growth programs. The drawback, however, is that on occasion a small percentage of participants are not able to cope with the insights they gain. The experience is too psychologically demanding; instead, defenses are triggered, and participants react negatively.

Finally, these programs provide an element of risk taking, and therefore energy, that the other approaches do not. While there is no established research to argue this point, my own experience tells me that learning can be magnified by risk-oriented experiences that challenge us either to act in new ways or to see the world vividly in ways we have not before. Such experiences have an impact when we have success experiences (in other words, when we succeed in the new behavior or with the new worldview) or when we have failure experiences from which we are willing to actively learn (not failures that we choose to ignore or in which we cannot see positive revelations). Simple skill building or conceptual training cannot offer this dynamic. For this reason, I believe that the personal growth programs make an important contribution to leadership training. In conclusion, the power of the personal growth approaches is that they directly challenge us to examine our most deeply felt emotions and most entrenched values. And if leadership is in part the emotional manifestation of one's passionate interests and aspirations, then this is where a significant portion of training must take place.

The Conceptual Approaches

As mentioned in earlier chapters, one school of thought on leadership training goes as follows: leadership is a complex art and one that is poorly understood. Therefore, the best we can hope to do with training is to create an awareness of the key ideas. With that awareness, managers can begin a lifelong process of learning to be leaders. Introducing managers to the key concepts behind leadership is thus the most advantageous use of a training seminar. This is an extreme position on the potential impact of leadership training, yet one that is implicitly endorsed by a majority of university programs. Our universities are primarily teaching leadership by imparting a conceptual understanding of the phenomenon.

We discovered that indeed simple, powerfully presented, single models of leadership could have an impact on behavior. Participants in these (and other) programs tended to focus on one or, less frequently, two key ideas of a model. Some described how the concept of vision had moved them to alter their organizational goals and to incorporate more futuristic aims. Others, who focused on the idea of inspiring, experimented with inspirational activities at the office. In one program, an executive commented on how the idea of "commitment" altered his goals: "I learned that leadership is essentially commitment. And that a passion for something is the key to commitment. It is a simple idea, but one that really helped me understand what I needed to do to ultimately become a leader."

To have a positive impact, a concept-oriented program

must be based on several important design factors. First, the program's leadership model should be relatively straightforward and should employ simple, memorable descriptions of each element; for example, "inspiring a shared vision" and "modeling the way" (The Leadership Challenge). This simplicity and phrasing allows for greater memory retention after the program.

Second, each element of the model needs to be supported with films, case studies, or exercises to illustrate the associated behaviors. Participants are able to connect the ideas with actual behaviors and to experiment with them. Many of the characters in both the films and case studies should be midlevel managers, not "bigger than life" leaders, allowing further grounding of ideas in peer role models.

In addition, outdoor-adventure experiences and skill-building exercises need to be employed as supplementary vehicles for grounding and practicing the behaviors associated with each element of the model. I believe these are critical in the success of any conceptually oriented program. Ideas in themselves can be quite powerful, but individuals often require an emotional experience to shift an idea from the intellectual level to a deeper understanding and then into action (a key idea of the personal growth programs). The following quote from the executive who spoke about commitment captures this important connection:

> If you have commitment, you will find a way. I knew I was not committed to what I was doing. I was stalling in my career on something I was not committed to. . . . I wanted to find a place where I could make a commitment. In the seminar, I realized that the reason for my dissatisfaction was that I was not motivated by making money and profits. Seeing people who were dedicated to this made me realize that I was not. There were other things that motivated me.
>
> We had an exercise where we had to give a Martin Luther King style speech. I stood up and tried to convince everyone at the seminar what my

vision for the company was. I sensed that it was
lacklustre. There was a very low response to the
question of who would be interested in following
my vision. I realized I was really not committed
to what I was projecting. That exercise drove home
powerfully ths idea of commitment. I knew I had
to do something!

What we see in this case is the concept of commitment
being connected to leadership experientially. At the onset of the
course, the executive learns intellectually the importance of commitment to a personally meaningful objective and its link to the
idea of leading. It is not, however, until the speech exercise that
he realizes quite profoundly that he himself does not possess the
commitment to his company's objectives to foster strong leadership. The experience then grounds the concept in emotional glue.
It will also encourage him to seek the services of a career consultant some six months later. As a result, he is today in a new
industry to which he is highly committed.

I believe that we have downplayed the importance of ideas
and concepts in training in recent years, perhaps as a backlash
against MBA programs (with accusations that they are too theory driven to be useful). Yet what we found was that ideas and
concepts were critically important in framing the notion of
leadership in participants' minds — especially when distinctions
were made between leadership and managership. This awareness-building provided the important first step in behavior development and change. Alone, however, it is not sufficient.

The Feedback Approaches

Ideally, one might assume, feedback should play a vital role in
helping managers identify the strong and weak points of their
leadership style. Our research results, however, were puzzling
because they indicated that feedback often had less impact than
we had expected.[3] Only in a very few cases did managers describe feedback as significantly enhancing their leadership skills.
Factors within the individual and outside the programs played

major roles in mitigating the contribution of feedback. Before we explore why feedback may not always work as effectively as expected, let us first look at those who felt it had a positive impact.

Participants who felt positively about the role of feedback in leadership development described themselves as in one of two situations. The first group were individuals who received feedback that powerfully contradicted their self-image on several dimensions of importance to them. At the same time, these individuals were motivated to examine what feedback told them was perceived as ineffective behavior. This "shock" led them to seriously examine their behavior and make concerted efforts to learn new, more effective behavior. The following is a representative comment: "I feel that the program had an enormous impact on me, and as a result, I have changed my style of leading. From the leaderless group exercises and the feedback I received, I became very aware of negatives in how I interact with others. I was surprised to see how I tend to turn people off by being too control oriented and aggressive. Since the Center's program, I now bite my tongue before speaking, and I give my subordinates a lot more latitude. I am supervising some very senior managers now and realize I don't need to be standing over their shoulders. My subordinates tell me that I am less controlling and that they like my more easygoing style."

Being motivated to reflect on one's behavior and to want to change are critical aspects of development; there were numerous participants who received negative feedback but chose to ignore it. Their reasons: some said they simply had no desire to lead, so why bother; others said that organizational forces got in the way; others said they were too old to change, and so on.

The second group who benefited from feedback were individuals who received highly favorable feedback, which came to them as a surprise. Generally, these were younger managers who were still uncertain about their effectiveness in a leadership role. The surprisingly positive feedback led to greater self-confidence, which in turn translated into more initiative and risk taking back on the job. The following comment captures this experience: "My subordinates' evaluations were way more positive than I had expected. This raised my confidence a lot. When I returned to work, I felt renewed, especially about my job. I was so encouraged that I began to implement new ideas and set up 'a development by objectives' program with my salespeople. I now find I am just more confident about myself at work and am a lot less anxious about how I present myself and my ideas. I am also more effective at motivating subordinates."

But these represent the minority of cases. Most participants in programs using formal feedback instruments felt that the feedback affirmed or validated what they already knew. Unlike the ones who described great benefits, these individuals felt that there were no surprises. Among them, however, quite a number reported choosing to improve one or two behaviors back on the job. Again, some representative comments:

> When I returned from the program, I made it a practice to consult much more often with my subordinates and peers. So now we have more frequent informal meetings. I also used to see many situations and tasks as essentially similar and I expected others to handle previously successful situations without hesitation. Now I realize this approach was too simplistic. Situations are not frequently so similar, and I am more sensitive to the fact that others will see those differences.

> Now I go out of my way to be more appreciative of others' work and make visible signs of that appreciation. I also work much harder on creating an environment of joint responsibility for decisions at work. I am giving subordinates more information as well.

We learned that participants tended to focus on only one or two areas of feedback as their development goals, even those who claimed the highest benefits from it. So, for example, a participant might receive feedback for poor active listening along with perhaps six other managerial or leadership skills. Instead of consciously working on all seven, the person would "remember" one to work on. I believe this happens for two important reasons.

The first is relatively obvious: the human mind has a difficult time actively storing and working on multiple behavioral changes at the same time, so it simplifies the task by focusing on one or two at a time. Second, some behavioral changes require a fundamental shift in one's psychological being—something that no seminar is likely to provide (in terms of the required follow-up support and guidance). So we gravitate to those behavioral changes that require little or no fundamental shifts in our psychological makeup.

For example, I discovered from the feedback I received that I needed to be more effective in conflict management, that I relied too heavily on a coaching leadership style, and that I was inconsistent in keeping others informed. Of these three areas, none came as a surprise. However, on my return to the job, I did focus on changing one of them. As mentioned earlier, I had not been doing an adequate job of keeping my secretary informed of my schedule; this was the area of negative feedback that I chose to work on. The other two behaviors would have required significant changes, both in my psychological character and in my work environment. Both were the results of years of family dynamics or of my occupation; conflict was never managed well in my family, and my role as a teacher consistently ingrained the coaching style as most effective with students. My mind, therefore, gravitated to the area of feedback that was psychologically the easiest of the three to implement.

Not surprisingly, however, most participants described a sincere desire to work on changing certain ineffective behaviors; however, they found that their desire dissipated soon after the program ended. Why, we asked. Some of the responses were the classic problems described in the training research; others were more surprising.

First, we learned that participants often reported feedback overload; that is, that the array of feedback instruments and the quantity of feedback in general were simply too much to digest. In the Center for Creative Leadership program, only four instruments could generally be recalled by name: the Myers-Briggs Type Indicator, the Firo-B, the Kirton Inventory, and the Leadership Style Inventory. Of these, the Myers-Briggs was usually the only one that was consistently recalled and was certainly the most popular in terms of being used to understand one's own behavior or that of others.

One effective means of countering feedback overload employed by the Center for Creative Leadership, however, was the two- to three-hour session with a staff psychologist who reviewed and integrated all the feedback learning from the course. This was described as the most powerful course experience for the majority of participants in that program.

A second and related problem with feedback was often focus. In some leadership courses, much of the feedback has to do with managerial skills rather than leadership. A clear distinction is often not drawn between the two. Further, priorities may not be outlined; for example, the skills that should be priorities for the development of a young manager's career should be clearly differentiated from the skills a senior executive needs. Unfortunately, most public training programs do not have the luxury of tailoring their programs to specific levels because they must appeal to a range of managerial levels.

We discovered, in addition, that individuals sometimes found instrument feedback too one-dimensional to be applicable in their experiences at home. It was simply interesting documentation. Other times, instrument measurements were perceived as less than meaningful. For example, some "leadership" instruments measured dimensions that were so global or vague that it was difficult to translate them into hands-on behaviors. As well, if an individual's ratings were positive or even at the median, they often did not encourage or motivate the participant to actively develop the identified skill areas.

Instrument feedback seemed most powerful when a particular behavior (on which the participant had already received instrument feedback) was actually experienced and witnessed during a program exercise. This allowed individuals to see themselves performing the specific behaviors and consciously "feel" the impact in the moment. Otherwise, we found that feedback from respected peers and facilitators (with the notable exception of the Myers-Briggs Type Indicator and occasionally one or two other instruments) had a greater impact than feedback from instruments in encouraging reflection and changing behavior.

In a few programs, we found that feedback was not always accompanied by sufficient opportunities for participants to experiment with new behaviors. For example, feedback might encourage a participant to try to be a more effective listener, but then the program would provide few or no skill-building exercises in active listening. Sometimes, so many behaviors are measured that it would be impossible to cover them all in a seminar. Moreover, few of the organizations to which participants returned had any follow-up program. In one rare case, a company hosted a one-day workshop in which participants talked about their experiences, but it provided no further support experiences.

In addition, participants reported giving up on their efforts to change because of a lack of coaching opportunities back on the job. I believe this lack of follow-through mechanisms is perhaps the greatest obstacle to feedback's having an important impact (this is well documented in the research literature).[4] For example, many participants talked about lack of support from their bosses. In the few cases where bosses or other co-workers themselves had been to the same program, there was a greater sense of support and motivation for changing one's behaviors. These statements are cases in point: "My direct supervisor and his supervisor have both attended the program. This has provided a strong support system for me on my return." "It was very helpful that all the managers and division directors had gone through the experience already. They could understand my changed perspective, appreciate it more, and support me."

In conclusion, feedback, in theory, should be most effective in leadership development as a guide to behaviors that need development; for example, feedback can effectively highlight negative or ineffective behaviors that detract from leadership ability and draw attention to skill areas that are underdeveloped. Just as significantly, it can be used to improve confidence and promote initiative by confirming strengths (especially those that are not fully recognized by the individual).

However, I have seen feedback instruments used most successfully in leadership development by consultants who have ongoing coaching relationships with managers or executives, and who employ instruments to guide those individuals' behavior and to update them on their progress. The validity of this approach appears supported by our own research, which shows that face-to-face feedback from a credible and trusted source (for example, a staff psychologist or consultant) seems to have the highest level of acceptance (with the exception of a very few instruments).

It is also clear that feedback needs to be focused on and designed around behaviors that individuals believe are important for their effectiveness. Secondly, surprises often seem to have a great impact because they challenge one's worldview. Finally, feedback instruments are static by nature; exercises that involve the behaviors that are being measured can be powerful grounding experiences.

What can we then realistically expect from a feedback-oriented approach to leadership development? Its added value is in sensitizing individuals to areas where their competencies are weak and in building confidence through very positive evaluations. The ultimate determining factor, however, is the individual's motivation to change a behavior, and this is determined by a wide range of factors, both within the individual and outside — largely beyond the context and control of any short-term program.

The Skill-Building Approaches

The attractiveness of the skill-building approaches is that they attempt to actually make leadership into a practical, teachable reality. By necessity, they demystify leadership; leadership cannot be too complex a concept or too deeply personal if it can be taught. Rather, it must embody concrete experiences that can be replicated. A skill-building approach demands that leadership abilities be broken down into actual mechanical processes that you and I can perform. Are these assumptions reasonable?

Well, it is clear that there are indeed certain skills of leadership (even under today's conceptions) that are learnable. For example, one skill that many participants appear to have acquired from several programs is the ability to recognize others' accomplishments in a proactive manner, which is one form of rewarding. I believe the primary reason this skill has been so effectively disseminated is that it is relatively easy to learn. As such, it lends itself to skill-building efforts. Without question, certain aspects of communicating and of motivating lend themselves to being taught. The success of leadership training programs, then, depends on whether they focus on the teachable skills or on the more complex, perhaps less trainable ones.

Second, most of the skill-building approaches rely on a single model of leadership to clearly convey their message. We discovered that this use of a single model appears to be a powerful approach because it helps participants remember key ideas about leadership. When multiple models are used, practically no one remembers them five to six months after the program has ended.

In addition, skill-building courses typically employ feedback instruments and peer feedback to help participants see where they stand relative to each of the behavioral dimensions of the model they are learning. As noted earlier, the feedback instrument forces managers to become conscious of their strengths and weaknesses around each dimension. For example, in the case of my research assistant who attended the Forum workshop, the feedback from the program caused her to spend considerable time reflecting on certain elements of her style.

Since the skill-building approaches rely on skills that are teachable, participants have concrete experiences upon which to measure their capabilities. Leadership is not a glamorous or distinct concept; rather it is a person's ability, for instance, to include something inspiring in business communications.

The skill-building approaches, however, present several difficulties. For one, they require greater commitment from organizations than, say, awareness-building approaches (for example, a conceptual program). Participants actually learn tangible skills that in theory are applicable in their organizations. On returning to their organizations, participants usually discover that their skill retention and ability to experiment depends directly on opportunities to practice and on active support from their work group. If neither are forthcoming within a relatively short period of time, the skills they have learned are likely to be discarded and forgotten. For this reason, training is more effective if intact work groups with their superiors attend the same program. They support and reinforce each other's skill-building efforts.

The transfer of skills back to the workplace, then, becomes a critical factor in the effectiveness of these programs. On the training organization's side, care must be taken to ensure that the experiences that are used as "metaphor experiences" are sufficiently realistic. For example, can we as participants clearly draw links between building model cars in a leadership exercise and what we might be doing back at the office to mobilize subordinates? Will the exercise sufficiently duplicate real-time leadership experiences in terms of the complexity and skills required? In many cases, participants find it difficult to draw links between exercises and work experiences. For this reason, training programs must constantly push participants to see and describe the possible connections between the exercises and their work experiences. The less personally relevant the exercise (either in terms of work or personal life), the more we found that boredom and apathy set in amongst participants. This is a major problem area for the skill-related programs because it is difficult to duplicate "back home" leadership situations with much realism.

A third difficulty for these programs is time. To truly learn a skill, an individual needs to spend considerable time with it, learning the basic ideas, experimenting, being coached, receiving feedback, and then continuing with experimentation and refinement. Most skill-building programs attempt to cover several major skill areas in a matter of days. So, for example, they may teach inspirational speaking skills in a morning and then move on to motivational skills in the afternoon. The next day is spent on vision, and so on. In reality, a few hours is far too little time to learn a skill.[5] Organizations and training companies are both under time and resource constraints; as a result, most of these skill-building approaches end up becoming awareness-building approaches. Participants must fend for themselves after they finish these programs, and seek out opportunities to practice these skills. A four- or five-day program can introduce the basics of a skill to participants, but cannot truly develop it for most of them.

An additional problem of skill-building approaches is that they may create unrealistic expectations around certain skills. For example, as I have mentioned before, certain leadership skills are far more complex than we realize. Let us take vision. From preliminary studies, we know that a leader's ability to envision goals is actually a complex process. Events stretching as far back as childhood may influence its origins. Further, it requires not only a special sensitivity to market forces but also awareness of constituents' needs — two characteristics that cannot be acquired overnight. Timing and luck also play an important part — something, again, that no seminar can offer or teach. Consequently, these skills are learned largely through important work experiences, not through a day's exposure to visioning skills.[6]

Finally, organizations tend to send their junior or mid-level managers to skill-building programs. The more senior managers often assume that they already possess such skills or they simply do not have the time to attend. As a result, a discrepancy evolves between the two levels. Because the senior team may not have been involved in such programs, they have little knowledge of the actual skill areas in which their junior managers are being trained. As a result, they are not as likely to recognize and actively reward and promote these skills when their returning subordinates try to put them into use. Other times, bosses may feel threatened by newly empowered subordinates and stifle their new orientation. Frustration builds among the junior managers, and the new skills are often abandoned for the old ways. It is therefore critical that somehow senior managers be actively involved in the program. Ideally, senior managers should have participated in such programs before the programs are administered wholesale to their organizations.

In conclusion, the skill-building approaches should be the most effective of all because they are under the highest expectations to produce tangible results. And with some leadership skills, this can be the case. The difficulty is that many of the skills currently associated with leadership are quite complex, and a three- or five-day program offers little time to truly develop these in lasting ways. Back on the job, the workings of the organization and the manager's daily life-style may further erode his or her initial efforts to implement skills. Awareness development may be a more realistic expectation for program outcome than actual in-depth skill development.

Conclusion

What can we conclude from this survey of the various approaches to leadership development? Foremost, it should be clear that to be effective, leadership training must incorporate elements of all four approaches: personal growth experiences, conceptual development, feedback, and skill building. Each integrates and builds upon the other.

Secondly, in the majority of cases, one should expect that training's primary role will be in awareness-building. Programs offer too little time for mastery of actual leadership skills or for kindling new motivation to lead. However, it is reasonable to expect that participants can intellectually learn key distinctions between managing and leading as well as some of the behaviors associated with each function. From feedback, they may also acquire insight into the presence or absence and the strength or weakness of these very behaviors in themselves.

Ultimately though, the encouragement and development of leadership skills rests with the individual's own motivation and talent and with the receptiveness of their organizations to support and coach such skills. This leaves a lot to chance. Practicing new behaviors requires willpower, patience, and persistence — difficult in the face of a busy day. In addition, subordinates and superiors expect a certain stability in a manager's behavior; even a positive change may threaten that image of stability. More significantly, many organizations are simply not prepared for leadership. Conformity is more important to them than vision and risk taking.

From the viewpoint of participants, there are additional difficulties. Not all adults can recognize and challenge their own assumptions. Some individuals are incapable of turning learning experiences into awareness because of their intellectual ability and defenses. For others, there may be intellectual awareness without action. Only a segment of the population may be able to gain awareness and then act. Moreover, some people may simply lack the will to change, to improve, to become leaders. And some may have very profound psychological problems that prevent them from ever leading.

Realistically, then, we might expect that a well-designed leadership program could result in something roughly like the following: (1) no behavioral change and little enhanced awareness for perhaps 10 to 20 percent of participants, (2) an expanded conceptual understanding of leadership for another 30 to 40 percent, (3) some positive though incremental behavioral change (in addition to a conceptual understanding) for an additional 25 to 30 percent, and (4) significant positive behavioral change for 10 percent. If a program can enhance the leadership abilities of just these percentages alone, I believe it is worth the time and expenditure. I also believe, however, that the potential could be higher with better preselection of participants and more powerful educational experiences. In the concluding chapter, I will describe several new approaches that might heighten the effectiveness of leadership training in the future.

The rest of this chapter is devoted to a case study of an individual who falls into that 10 percent of participants who experience a major behavioral change in a leadership training program that enhances their leadership effectiveness. This individual's history sheds light on interventions that are transforming. He was a participant in the Center for Creative Leadership's LeaderLab program (which I describe in Chapter Nine and which I observed but did not participate in). The program combines elements of all four approaches with some balance and involves two one-week-long sessions separated by three months. The separation between course sessions allows both participants and trainers an opportunity to observe behavioral changes that occur after the first week's work. Ted (his name is disguised) was described by participants, trainers, and himself as having undergone a major behavioral change.

Ted is a thirty-one-year-old fast-track manager in a large

financial services firm. His current position is considered very
advanced for a manager of his age. While Ted has strong leadership potential, he has had serious interpersonal problems that
alienate him from others, especially peers and underperforming subordinates. A sense of superiority led him to quickly
prejudge situations and people. In addition, his style could be
intimidating when he perceived limited competence. These have
been the largest blocks to his ability to lead others effectively.

Ted's performance appraisals have always been high, the
glaring exception being the problem of interpersonal dynamics.
Over three years, Ted's superior provided consistent, open feedback concerning those problems. Ted accepted his superior's
observations and attempted to behave differently, but, as he explains it, change would last for a period of two weeks and then
reverse itself:

> I now realize that at the time I was working on the
> symptoms, not the causes. I would receive nega-
> tive feedback, try some new behaviors, succeed
> briefly, and then fall back into my old behavior.
> I wanted to change. I knew it was a career blocker —
> not in the sense of losing my job or making less
> money, but in getting ahead and being an effec-
> tive leader. I came to the LeaderLab program with
> a long list of things to work on. When I received
> my feedback (negative) from subordinates and peers
> at LeaderLab, nothing there was a surprise. I knew
> I had this problem. My wife also has been very clear
> with me about how I affect people's feelings. As well,
> when I was twenty, I was a unit head at a summer
> camp. The director gave me a three-page review
> at the end of the summer. He explained how or-
> ganized I was but that my interpersonal relations
> with staff were negative. So it's been a problem I
> have known about for a long time.

Ted came to the LeaderLab experience with several specific behavioral changes that he wished to make: (1) to no longer

intimidate subordinates,(2) to no longer put peers in a position of "looking stupid," (3) to delegate more, and (4) to make his staff feel that he was interested in their input. Feedback at LeaderLab confirmed his weakness on all these dimensions.

Ted felt impatience bordering on contempt during the first several days of LeaderLab, and on the second day he made what he felt was an inadvertently insulting remark to the instructor, a remark that implied ignorance on the instructor's part and superior knowledge on Ted's part. His interpersonal weaknesses were coming through on the course. He began to feel that the course offered him little of value. Later this would prove to be his defenses acting out and in turn causing interpersonal problems.

On the fifth day of the LeaderLab program, all participants typically meet with an individual called a process advisor. The advisor's aim is to help participants with "back home" planning as they prepare to implement what they have learned at LeaderLab. The advisor also stays in touch with the participant for three months after the program ends, to help facilitate change. The advisor in Ted's case was a clinical psychologist. The following transcript of an interview with Ted and his advisor, Mary, explains what happened during their first interview on day five:

Mary: It's important to know beforehand that Ted approaches things with a sense of wonder, of curiosity. So he's open, to a good degree.

Ted: I came to LeaderLab with the intention of getting something out of this experience. I had an expectation of sequential learning. Learn a model, get some data, and then understand it. Wednesday evening we went on a nature walk to find an object that depicts what we want to represent our leadership when we return home. I thought to myself that that was not going to make me a better leader. So I was in a real cynical mood. It was the next morning in my interview with Mary that things started to happen.

Mary: Before meeting Ted, I had read his biography, his sense of purpose statements, and I had reviewed his feedback from

subordinates, peers, and superiors. Two things struck me when
I read through this material. The first was that he was still very
young, and yet he had reached a very high level. I also had a
sense of someone in a hurry. I remember at one point asking
him, "What's the big hurry?" He already had a lot of accomplishments—Eagle Scout at fourteen, and so on. He seemed in a
big push to prove something.

    I sensed he had a fear of failing, of looking incompetent.
He has been this bright kid on the block as a financial analyst
who now was in an executive position. There was a fear that
he might not be seen as the best in the new position. On the
surface, you can develop skills. But when you reach a certain
level you will not progress until you face your deeper blocks.
You have to face your issues of self-worth. Also you have to
know what you really want. When I asked Ted what he really
wanted, he was struck by the question. He said, "I don't know.
I need to think about it."

    Later that day, Ted would record in a personal diary the
emotional impact of his meeting with Mary:

    My time with Mary today was truly amazing. A
    lot came together. I nearly broke down in tears.
        Using your whole self—complete with the
    emotional side—appears to be what I need.
        Why am I in a hurry?
        What is there behind the locked door of my
    childhood? How much energy did I use to keep that
    door closed? Do I want to open it? Perhaps it would
    be better left closed.
        How can I say it strongly enough? What a
    study in contrast? I had made a judgment about
    how much I would get out of my session with Mary,
    based on my original impression of her as "touchy
    feely" sort.
        Why do I make judgments about people in
    such a fast manner? Where does that tendency come
    from?

How do I achieve my vision of a balanced leadership style where I maintain a sense of humor and don't beat on people? There seem to be two ways:

A. Modify my actions. Specific things I do/don't do. Set up a reward/punishment system to reinforce this.
B. Open the door that exists between the two compartments of logic and emotion.

I knew about the first option before coming here. What about the second?

I know I am cognitive. Why do I only nurture that part of my brain? Certainly, this is what was encouraged when I was a child. Emotions were suppressed. My father always kept himself under control when my mother went off the deep end.

Mary explains more fully this connection between Ted's personality and his parent's behavior and how Ted was uniquely able to channel his insight into a personal transformation:

He had had a very extreme childhood. His mother was very unstable. His father had to suppress emotions in order to cope with Ted's mother. His model for emotions was someone losing control. In the interview, in questioning this part of his past, he had all his feedback notes on the desk in front of him. Looking at them, he said, "I thought this was what I really needed to work on, but what I now realize is that I really need to work on why I have so compartmentalized my feelings."

It was such an emotional insight for him that he started to cry. It put the rest of the week in perspective. He's in reality a feeling person, and at home he's allowed that to occur, but not at work. The realization that he was like his father in that behavior was a critical and jarring insight. He also had his intelligence going for him. He is clearly one of the most intelligent individuals in the program to date. As well, he was in a new situation back at work. So he had no history with the people with whom he was working. The danger was that he had to get his portfolio in shape within six months, and he felt he had to effect a major restructuring. The danger, then, was that he would give in to feeling pressured again and revert to old behaviors. But he resisted this in several ways. In meetings at work, he was deliberately modest and low-key, which was very different for him. He delegated more. He asked people their opinions. When you're known for being fast and having the answers, that is very difficult to do.

Ted's case is instructive as to what can happen in an effective leadership training program. In this case, Ted's leadership ability was being blocked by his poor interpersonal dynamics (which, I suspect, is the case for many potential leaders). This weakness hampered his ability to motivate and align others. The cause for this interpersonal ineffectiveness, however, was rooted in childhood and not consciously known to Ted. As a result, its impact was more pervasive than Ted could appreciate, which explains why Ted's earlier changes lasted only weeks. Through his experience in the program, Ted came to realize why he feels so driven to control and to prove himself. The revelation that this is his inner child's reaction to parental dynamics has allowed him to see that such behavior is not needed in his work environment. The emotional experience that accompanied this insight shocked him into essentially a new view of himself that helped Ted understand his surface behavior. This new self-knowledge permitted him to relinquish the previously unconscious need to maintain control and to prove himself and facilitated, in unison with his willingness to experiment, a change in behavior.
    A crucial aspect of Ted's case is his motivation to examine his behavior and to change, a motivation that comes from within himself and from pressures from his boss. Further, he possesses a strong intellect and the ability to reflect, and the capacity for effective interpersonal skills is present but dormant in work situations. In addition, he began a new job immediately after the first LeaderLab session, so that he was freed from others' preconceptions of what his behavior would be. Finally, into this process came a program design that forced self-reflection

and provided feedback. A highly skilled process advisor was the final catalyst; through a series of thought-provoking questions, she triggered a pivotal and behavior-changing insight. The process advisor then followed up over the next three months to help Ted with behavior change. All these positive events reinforced each other to facilitate Ted's change. The end result was a transformation in his approach to leading:

> Today, I ask rather than tell. I reflect. I am willing to let decisions go in directions that were not my original conclusion. I don't interrupt people as much. I'm not as quick to judge others. I help nurture others, asking how they feel about their jobs, what they want. So today good people want to work with me. I am also now beginning to build teams. I feel I am on the road to becoming a much more effective leader than I was before.

The absence of one or two of the factors described might have earlier precluded this transformation in Ted. Few participants are likely to have so many positive forces coming together at any one time as Ted did. For this reason, I would argue that at best only 10 percent of participants in an effective training program will experience significant change.

This example also highlights why the personal growth dimensions of a program are, I believe, among the greatest levers that formal training can apply in developing leadership ability, which is why we need to spend more time understanding them. Potentially, they address the inner side of an individual, which is where leadership may ultimately spring from or where it is blocked. These approaches are the riskiest, since they deal with human emotions and involve psychological interventions. Nonetheless, I believe there are many "Teds" out there who have the potential to be fine leaders but have interpersonal handicaps—and such programs can help. Much design work remains to be done, however, if leadership training is to become a significant organizational force for helping potential leaders realize their potential. In Chapter Nine, we will look at new program designs and company experiments that can heighten training's impact.

Chapter Nine

Beyond Myers-Briggs and Rope Climbing: The Future of Leadership Training

*C*hange is the only constant in life.

— Anonymous

Having looked at the current approaches to teaching leadership skills, we now must stand back and ask ourselves whether these approaches will take us successfully into the future. I believe that they will not. I believe that radical changes will ultimately have to occur in both the content and the process of leadership training if corporations of the future are to ensure an adequate supply of leaders for themselves. In addition, corporations will have to make some serious changes in themselves.

While I believe that many of today's programs have done an excellent job of building awareness, there are several important elements that are missing in all of them. If we go back to the idea that leadership education is at least two decades old, we have to ask ourselves why we do not see more leaders today. I have yet to hear of an organization complaining of too many leaders. So why is it that after so much time and money there is not more evidence of leadership?

First, awareness training is not enough. It is important,

but not enough. Psychotherapists tell us that insight into one's behavior is never sufficient to transform an individual. The same law applies to leadership training. Studying leadership is no substitute for leading. And while the awareness-building phase has been an important step toward meeting new demands for greater leadership, it must be followed by a phase of deep skill development. Most managers by now understand the distinctions between managing and leading, thanks to a flood of seminars, books, and press coverage on the subject.

But this brings us to a second problem facing today's training programs—time. How can a three- or five-day program have a significant impact, in terms of developing lasting skills? Clearly it cannot. It would make better sense to send managers to an intensive three-day program focusing on the development of one leadership skill. But because we are still in the awareness-building phase, the "wine tasting" (a taste of every skill) approach dominates. For a moment, however, suppose that we became even more serious about training and began sending employees to longer courses or sending them more frequently. We would still face the problem of the training organizations themselves.

Most training organizations are now very skilled at awareness building, but they are weaker, I would argue, in the actual development of lasting leadership abilities for their participants. In part, this is because they have built their expertise around awareness. In part, it is because training organizations and society itself do not completely understand the mechanics of adult education. For example, I am convinced that the personal growth approaches could be significantly more powerful than they are, but many of their designers do not fully appreciate the mechanics of their own techniques or, more accurately, do not know how to package the experiences they offer in more effective ways.

But then, let us say that the training organizations were able to develop some truly powerful experiences that enhanced leadership ability. Would that be enough? No—because the most important culprits responsible for leadership training not being as effective as it could be are the organizations who use the programs. Deep down, many organizations do not want more

leaders. They prefer managers — and for a simple reason: they
are a known and controllable quantity. Leaders are not. They
take initiative, they challenge the status quo, they encourage
followings. For many companies, this is a frightening prospect.
A five-day outside leadership program is a safe alternative to
cultivating leadership from within. An organization can show
an interest in leadership without taking a deeper responsibility
for its successful realization.

But even the organizations that are sincere about leadership development face a factor peculiar to leadership training
that causes problems for them. Unlike the quality movement,
which has been enormously successful in terms of training in-
vestments and returns, the value of leadership is difficult to measure. How can you accurately gauge the "returns" on a leadership training program? The answer is that you cannot. This
dilemma makes it extremely difficult for companies to commit
large sums of money to something from which they will see no
immediate, tangible results. We want to see what we pay for.
Leadership is an elusive long-term investment, especially for
a society that often looks only to the next quarter or the next year.

Let us say that finally, however, we find an organization
truly committed to leadership development. What would we have
to do to make training work? First, the focus would have to move
to the more teachable skills. For example, certain rewarding techniques and motivational speaking skills can be taught, as we
have seen. Intense skill development in these areas should be
our focus. While we would continue to make people aware of
the other more complex skills, such as vision, we should accept
the fact that our efforts here will be largely awareness building
and not be disappointed if they do not translate into real skills.
Perhaps one day a participant will have an opportunity to use
the lessons on vision, but program time should mainly be devoted to teaching concrete, observable, measurable skills.

We also need to make more extensive use of the personal
growth approaches. They particularly offer us powerful tools
to help managers overcome ineffective interpersonal behaviors
that block their leadership ability; to foster changes in managers'
worldviews, opening them to the possibility of greater vision;

and to build managers' self-esteem and confidence and in turn encourage them to take the initiatives associated with leading.

In part, leadership is passion. It is a passion for what we do, and it is a contagious passion. You cannot teach people to be passionate. An acting class might help, but a leader's passion more often comes from the heart and gut. So a "passion skills" course will not do. The key is for each person to find out what deeply interests him or her about their work. Of all the training approaches, the personal growth ones come the closest to addressing this issue. Equally important, the personal growth approaches "shake our boxes." They challenge our worldviews. And for some, they may provide important metaphors or ideas that can trigger new behavior. In all these cases, they force us to look inward to realize our potential. The problem is that they do it largely in a hit-or-miss fashion. The current approaches need more refinement. As well, with these approaches, companies have to assume the risk that some employees will realize their passions outside of the company, which could lead to discontentment or even to their departure.

As for the other formats, the conceptual approach will continue to be necessary as our notions of leadership shift with the times. Skill building will always have significant practical value in training if it focuses on teachable behaviors and goes for depth in individual skills. In addition, participants must be supported in the use of their new skills back in the office. Feedback approaches will remain important if they are designed around a few instruments, and feedback and coaching from credible individuals.

In addition, future programs will have to address the issue of new topics, new concerns. For example, the problems of supervising a culturally diverse work force or of managing a highly decentralized organization receive little or no coverage in the programs described in this book. Yet these are critical skill-development areas for the future.

Let us assume, however, that for the moment, the single greatest dilemma we face in leadership training is whether participants will retain their newfound insights and skills. What can be done by both training organizations and their clients to ensure that the seeds of leadership are cultivated? Course design and a new view toward leadership training as one of several complementary mechanisms in a company's overall leadership development strategy will be the keys. Let us start with course design.

Course Design

Course design, I believe, comprises three key elements that are necessary to ensure a lasting impact for training: multiple sessions, pre- and postcourse contact, and innovative class sessions. I will use the new LeaderLab program developed by Robert Burnside and Victoria Guthrie, at the Center for Creative Leadership in Greensboro, North Carolina, as one model of what future programs can do. This newly developed course came to my attention as we were completing our research. Following a preliminary round of telephone interviews with participants (which were very positive), I decided to observe the course and interview a current group of program participants.

Double Sessions

LeaderLab is built on the premise that a single, one-time course is insufficient to create and support lasting behavioral change. Instead, it starts with a six-day course, which is followed by a break of three months, and then a four-day follow-up course. In the first session, participants develop a leadership improvement program for themselves. This is implemented during the three-month interval. The final four-day course is an opportunity to review the progress of their plan and to modify it for the future. The Harvard Business School at one time offered a similarly designed program called Managing Organizational Effectiveness, and some in-company programs (such as one at Ford Motor Company) also incorporate elements of this design.

This multiple-session design creates a form of discipline for participants. For example, in several of the other courses I attended (which did not use multiple sessions), participants were asked to outline a series of leadership actions for their return to the job. In one case, they were joined in pairs, each participant being responsible for telephoning the other in three months to see how they were progressing on their plans. In another program, participants were mailed a copy of their in-course action plan by the training organization three to five months after the course, as a reminder. In neither case did most participants describe such follow-up procedures as highly effective.[1] Many forgot to call or forgot to follow through on their plans. In LeaderLab, however, participants felt accountable for their plans and were aware that they would be reexamining their progress in depth some three months later. This lent greater realism to the steps to be taken, in that they would be subject to scrutiny sometime later.

The course-break-course design also fosters greater reflection among participants because of the three-month period of experimentation and the later four-day review. Knowing that they must return and critique their plan keeps participants continually reflecting on their actions. Ideally, programs of the future would also include a one-year and possibly a two-year review. There is no doubt that implementing major changes requires more than a period of three months. The trade-off is the greater cost of such programs. But the idea of multiple sessions is not new or experimental. There are other more experimental mechanisms in LeaderLab that further reinforced commitment to behavioral change and experimentation — most important was a system of pre- and postcourse contact.

Pre- and Postcourse Contact

LeaderLab is centered around an examination of one's current leadership situation. To facilitate deeper reflection, precourse packets are provided to participants to help them analyze their situations objectively and critically. Each packet includes a variety of qualitative analyses that require participants to articulate their sense of purpose, their life experiences to date, and their current work situation, as well as fill out certain feedback instruments. Interestingly, a camera is also included in the package so that program members can visually capture the individuals and situations for which they are developing action plans during the course. The camera is a critical means of forcing participants to reflect more deeply and objectively. It is one thing to explain that your assistant is hotheaded and resists change, and another to explain her behavior when you have a photograph that shows her to be a charming and mature individual. The realism this kind of analysis commands is largely owing to participants developing a more complex understanding of the people and the issues they are facing.

The most important element in terms of pre- and post-course contact, however, is the process advisor. This individual is usually a staff psychologist who is versed in organizational issues. Their role as described by the Center is "one of coach, advisor, friend, cop, advocate, behavioral scientist. This person must continually prod and encourage the participant to move ahead, to address issues and blocks, to understand how blocks get in the way, and to help in strategizing ways to move them or confront them."[2]

The process advisor's objectives are to assist participants during the training to design their action plans and then to provide follow-up support. This support becomes particularly critical if participants are making behavioral changes that are not necessarily easy or comfortable for them. Contact with the process advisor starts a month or so before the program, with an introductory telephone call. In each of the two course sessions, there are individual meetings with the advisor, followed by monthly telephone contact during the three-month interim period and again, for two months, after the second session. The telephone contact allows the advisor to monitor the participant's progress and to help with trouble-shooting in areas where little progress appears to have been made. To further enhance the effectiveness of these telephone meetings, each participant keeps a daily learning journal, the contents of which are forwarded to the process advisor prior to each telephone contact. Thus the advisor can see the daily issues and concerns that the participant is facing. In addition, it forces participants to explore their situations in far greater depth, again encouraging greater learning.

During the two course sessions, the process advisors meet

with their assigned participants on the first day and in one-on-one two-hour sessions later in the week. For the later sessions, they serve as resources to help participants identify the leadership improvements they wish to make and to identify actions that participants must take to improve themselves. In addition, during the second course session, each process advisor meets in a group session with the three participants he or she has been assigned to. There the participants present accounts of their progress — the successes and the barriers. The group evaluates each report and identifies the major points; and then the information is presented to a full class session.

Further support and reinforcement for one's action plan comes in the form of change partners. In-course change partners consist of three-person teams who work together throughout the program. They function as a practice vehicle of involved peers for each other's leadership experiences. They must learn about each other and learn to work with one another. In many cases, they evolve into a support system for each other during the three-month back-home period.

Back-home change partners are people at the work site whom participants feel can assist them as they try to improve their leadership efforts. The program designers, Burnside and Guthrie, note that these back-home partners need to embody three qualities: "encouragement (someone to pat them on the shoulder and egg them on); wisdom (someone who had been through the changes similar to what the participant is attempting and knows their local situation); and truth (someone who will give them honest feedback about the impact of their changes). . . . Since no one person usually can provide all three things needed, the participant works with three or four people, getting at least one thing from each of them. This is often a difficult task, and is one tool the Process Advisor tries to help the participant get established during the three-month period."[3]

The change partners, in combination with a process advisor, provide an important missing link in leadership training: the coach. Until now, coaching might on rare occasion appear in the form of a manager back at the participant's organization who had attended a similar program and who enjoyed mentoring.

But from our own research, this rarely if ever happened. The coaching provided by training organizations typically ended the last day of each program since no formal after-course mechanisms often existed. LeaderLab, however, recognizes that if training is to play a truly developmental role, it must provide coaching mechanisms that extend beyond the course itself. In this case, the training organization assumes that responsibility rather the participant's organization (which would leave much more to chance). The question remains, however, whether even longer-term contact with an advisor is necessary to ultimately ensure the lasting development of leadership abilities initiated by a program. There is also the issue of the higher costs involved with program designs that provide such extensive follow-up. This is an expensive design feature.

Classroom Activities

One element of a more impactful education experience may be a series of experiences that challenge and expose a person's worldview. By shaking hidden or taken-for-granted assumptions, training can sometimes help people to see the necessity of behavioral change for themselves and of strategic changes for their organizations. In addition, such experiences can open up the emotional sides of an individual, which in turn may foster greater creative expression, personal empowerment, or more effective relational behavior. For this reason, the personal growth approaches have an appeal.

Other mediums, currently overlooked, may be useful in leadership training. For example, beyond traditional models, exercises, and simulations, we may wish to draw upon methods that develop the artistic dimensions of leadership, for "a leader uses more than words and intelligence. The tone of the voice and body language — even the gestures he or she chooses to use or not use — come into play. Thus, participants must . . . look at leadership as a performing art."[4] To respond to this need, LeaderLab employs acting sessions taught by a producer/actor/director (I am also aware that Kouzes and Posner have experimented with acting lessons in their seminars). They focus initially on key gestures that individual participants make in certain situations. The instructor provides feedback based on his or her observations of the participants' behavior during an opening simulation and other exercises. Suggestions are made as to which gestures and body language enhance the individual's effectiveness in leadership situations and which ones detract.

There are other sessions that break down traditions of talk and intellectualizing. Working with a family therapist, course members visually "sculpt" particular organizational problems that each participant is facing at work, using one another as figures in the sculptures. For instance, one individual was facing serious resistance to his plans from a boss. In a sculpture of the boss, another participant was placed in the position of posing with his hands against the body of the "sculptor." Subordinates are arranged pushing the "sculptor" from behind in support of the change. Other nuances are sculptured in to represent the different agendas each team member has in promoting the change, using hands, feet, faces, and so on. After sculpting the scenario as it is currently occurring, the "sculptor" assigns statements to each member of the sculpture and explores the reactions and emotions that go with the scene. Afterward, they must change the scenario into what they wish it to look like in the future. This helps participants envision and plan their "back-home actions." They then reorganize the sculpture, putting it back into its original form, and through gradual sculpting changes they "move" it to the desired future state. This exercise encourages participants to anticipate concretely the emotional issues they will face as they undertake action steps back home.

It is difficult to determine at this stage whether such experiments will foster greater leadership ability back at the office. From interviews we conducted with LeaderLab participants, it was, however, widely felt that such exercises were not only helpful but at times powerful. At the very least, these teaching innovations are important experiments in our attempts to access more of the individual's persona. They try to break beyond our rational sides — our stable worldviews — that usually do not permit much vision or creativity to emerge.

The use of unusual classrooms may be an additional source

source of innovation in class activities. For example, one executive leadership program experimenting with this idea is the Global Leadership Program developed by Professor Noel Tichy at the University of Michigan. What makes this program so special is that it attempts to teach an understanding of both global and strategic issues through action learning in special and highly relevant settings. For example, participants (executives from a variety of international companies) are taken in teams to Brazil, India, or China (locations vary with programs), where they begin a two-week study mission, identifying business opportunities in each country. They experience firsthand the dilemmas and opportunities of potential new markets. *The Bricker Bulletin* aptly describes the experience: "Affected by unanticipated political events, frustrated by bureaucratic red tape, or incapacitated by unfamiliar cuisine, the teams struggled to evaluate the long-term business potential of a foreign market while they were being forced to resolve cultural differences among team members. The teams toured businesses and met with corporate leaders and political officials, and, in order to better understand the real nature of the host country, they visited typical homes and local market places, traveling by public transportation."[5]

Learning by doing in unique classrooms such as these will increasingly become the educational wave of the future. The only barriers to their more widespread use will be the cost and the more complex logistics that are involved.

These three areas of course design — multiple sessions, advisory pre- and postcontact, and innovative teaching methods and classrooms — will prove to be important features of future programs. But creative and effective training programs will not be enough. There still remains the problem of what happens to participants when they return to their organizations. In the end, this is the soil onto which the seeds of leadership training must fall. If it is rocky, the effects of training are not likely to take hold. Let us look at what two organizations have been doing to give training a greater chance.

Leadership Training and Corporate Involvement

One of the great dilemmas facing leadership training today is the inability of corporations to integrate participants' insights into life back at the office. The tendency has been for companies to view training simplistically — to fail to see that leadership development is a long-term commitment and one that requires organizational mechanisms to sustain and integrate its effects. If training is ultimately to be effective, it must become one of several highly integrated elements of a gestalt of leadership development approaches to which organizations seriously commit.

The first step must be to customize programs to meet the specific needs of each company. For example, Ford Motor Company has instituted a middle management program entitled LEAD, which attempts to provide a cross-functional perspective of the company and the key roles and leadership challenges of middle managers. It begins with a six-day program examining issues around leadership, customer needs, quality issues, and the management of changes that apply to Ford and the automobile industry. During an interim period of six to eight months, managers apply what they have learned back on the job. A three-day follow-up session is then held wherein participants revisit their accomplishments and assess what they need to reinforce and what to correct. Numerous other companies are experimenting with such educational programs built around the company itself and its specific leadership needs.

As well, there have been attempts to maximize the impact of training by ensuring that a majority of managers and employees in a company attend programs. In this way, training becomes a powerful tool for socializing employees into the values and behaviors that are rewarded.

Several companies, however, have taken the process a step further and, as a result, have the potential to dramatically heighten the usefulness of training as a developmental experience. We will look at two companies in particular — General Electric and Levi Strauss — both of which are doing innovative experiments with leadership development.

General Electric:
A Step Further with Leadership Training

Perhaps no company in the world expends so much of its resources on corporate training as does the General Electric Company. Training at GE is seen as a pivotal element toward achieving the company's strategic objectives. The centerpiece for much of the company's training efforts is its Management Development Institute. Located twenty-five miles north of New York City, the center is known as "Crotonville," taking its name from the small Westchester County community where it is located. It is one of the oldest corporate residential education centers in North America.

Crotonville has a unique history in that senior leaders of the company have used it as a vehicle for corporatewide change.[6] When Ralph Cordiner became CEO in 1950, he implemented a new strategic shift for the company that decentralized the organization by product lines. As the shift was being made, a serious difficulty arose — the company lacked sufficient multifunctional general managers to run a decentralized company. Through the facilities of Crotonville, a major effort was launched to develop those skills with an advanced management program.

The next CEO, Fred Borch, saw the facility as a vehicle to introduce the concept of strategic planning to GE. Borch's successor, Reginald Jones, used Crotonville to expand the strategic planning effort and to improve inflationary accounting practices and cash management among company managers.

GE's most recent CEO, Jack Welch, is today using Crotonville as the educational centerpiece for a cultural transformation of the company. With an ambitious strategy of making all GE businesses either first or second in their markets, Welch set out to downsize, de-bureaucratize, and transform General Electric.

By the mid-1980s, in response to Welch's aims, Crotonville, under the direction of James Baughman, embodied a fundamental shift that was occurring in the management training world. The harsh competitive pressures of the 1980s had forced companies to reexamine the value of their educational programs. More importantly, businesses were grappling with the fact that much of what their employees were learning at training seminars did not seem to be transferring back to the workplace. Concepts often remained concepts. Cases often dealt with other companies or other industries. Attempts to transfer knowledge to the demands of specific jobs in specific companies were rare.

So by the 1980s, numerous programs underwent a shift to involve managers in analyzing actual company problems and devising action plans to solve them. Training became more results-oriented, with the programs designed to help managers implement actual business strategies and achieve company goals. Along with a handful of other companies, Crotonville led the way in this shift.

Curriculums were redesigned to emphasize "action learning."[7] The Crotonville curriculum now incorporated the study of actual GE business problems and their possible solutions. Since competitive pressures were demanding more and more teamwork across functional areas, learning now occurred in groups. Multifunctional teams of participants learned together. Since competition was occurring globally, learning now took place outside of North America. Teams of participants would grapple, for example, with strategic problems in Europe, with all their relevant cross-cultural issues.

At the core of these programs are consulting projects provided by GE businesses, seeking ideas in return for their cooperation. After reviewing background materials, training teams travel to the headquarters of their assigned businesses — domestic or abroad — to perform further diagnostic research. They have access to key managers and can review essential financial and marketing information as well as visit the field and customers. Drafts of their findings and recommendations are reviewed by outside consultants who identify gaps in the analyses and assist in mapping out strategies for overcoming resistance to the plans. The teams then present their recommendations to a senior group of executives from the businesses concerned. In follow-up sessions, participants learn from the various businesses about the successes and problems that their recommendations encountered as they were implemented.

An additional facet of GE's approach that is unique is the recognition that the leadership skills demanded by each level of the organization will be different from the next level. Crotonville has developed a systematic approach to this problem by positioning training programs at key developmental transitions in a manager's career.

Based on GE's value objectives, Crotonville's career model

for leadership development identifies key transition points in an individual's career. These are called "moments of opportunity"; they are times when a manager could be impacted by shared values and a realization of the leadership characteristics demanded by that particular transition point. From this, a pyramid of development stages was built. The process, however, is based on the assumption that recruitment and selection are crucial: good material entering at the bottom of the pyramid will emerge as exceptional material at the top.

The stage idea incorporates the notion that at each level a manager is faced with two leadership competency issues — scale and complexity. The scale issue revolves around the fact that each new level increases the number of individuals to be managed. So the salesperson who becomes a sales manager must manage several individuals, whereas before he or she managed none. From a leadership perspective, training addresses the question, Does this manager have the competency to do this? Can a senior manager running a plant of one thousand now manage a division of ten thousand? The second competency issue is complexity. As a manager moves up the hierarchy, the complexity of issues necessarily increases. Managing the problems of a unit on the manufacturing floor is a less complex challenge than managing the problems of an entire plant. So as a manager moves up, he or she must be able to address issues related to increasing scale and complexity.

The specific transition points are positioned around intersections where scale and complexity increase. Training is then targeted to synthesize past experiences at the previous level and to simulate the leadership demands that will present themselves at the new level. Each level is defined around a set of competencies demanded specifically by that point in the hierarchy. These competencies range from leadership and managerial skills to more specific functional and strategic knowledge.

Essentially, the system is based on the idea that critical competencies define each level and that these skills differentiate between mediocre and superior performers at each respective level. Training is then performed around the differentiators that are deemed teachable.

Integral to the process are competency ratings performed by peers and subordinates. So each participant receives direct feedback on his or her strengths and weaknesses for the new job level. Maximizing the effectiveness of this feedback is the fact that General Electric is in the unique position of having collected norms for all its participants at each level (some tens of thousands of managers have participated in the various programs). This database, combined with class norms, is used in the feedback process. The manager is then presented with data in graphic form that illustrate his or her strengths and weaknesses at their particular level. The feedback emphasizes areas of competency that are important for the manager's level but in which the individual shows low competence.

The value of a stage model of training is that managers are provided with broadening and skill-building experiences to address the new challenges that accompany each transition to a new level. It prepares participants for their future work and provides them opportunities to reflect and learn from their experiences in previous positions. In addition, it builds on research that has shown managers to be most receptive to new ideas and training at career transition junctures.

The Crotonville program ensures two strategic advantages for General Electric. It is a powerful mechanism for socializing company managers into General Electric's key values and norms. And it provides an opportunity for senior management to remain in touch with the organization — to sense its moods, skills, and so on. This is accomplished easily by involving senior managers in the educational programs as speakers or participants in question and answer periods. Through these sessions, they can sense the pulse of organization. Crotonville is not simply a training facility; it is a mechanism for inculcating values and gauging the organization's climate.

While General Electric's approach heightens the relevance and applicability of the training program, there must still be integrating or reinforcing mechanisms back in the organization. Otherwise, there is no guarantee that participants will use the new leadership skills. One company, Levi Strauss, is attempting to take the process that additional step further.

Levi Strauss & Co.:
Integrating Training with Organizational Factors

Recognizing that leadership training may not translate into actual behavioral change, Levi Strauss & Co. (LS&Co.) decided to experiment with organizational systems to support the process "back home." The reality of implementing such systems is extremely difficult, and I believe that Levi Strauss & Co. is still in an experimental phase. Nonetheless, their efforts are in the right direction. Levi Strauss & Co. is also an organization that has discovered that the cultivation of leadership is a never-ending process.

It is important to set the stage for LS&Co's approach to leadership development by providing some historical background. In many ways, the company's progress to date is the result of a change born out of crisis. Levi Strauss experienced phenomenal growth throughout the 1970s; sales increased from $350 million in 1970 to $2 billion in 1979. Jeans became one of the world's leading fashion statements. By the late 1970s and early 1980s, however, concerns about a stabilizing market for jeans led Levi Strauss & Co. to diversify. Through its purchase of Koracorp in the early 1980s, it acquired Koret of North America, Resistol, Oxford, Rainfair, and Fra-For. Then, the company acquired Frank Shorter Running Gear and signed licensing agreements with designers Perry Ellis, Andrew Feza, and Alexander Julian. The company began to reposition itself as a marketing and apparel company, not as a jeans manufacturer. This diversification strategy, however, was unsuccessful.

Robert Haas, the great-great-grandnephew of founder Levi Strauss, assumed the CEO position from Robert Grohman in 1984 and redirected the company's strategy of diversification to a "back to basics" one. The company narrowed its manufacturing focus to core products: jeans, jeans-related apparel, and selected casual wear. In 1985, Haas engineered a $1.65 billion leveraged buyout (LBO), the largest in American business history at the time. Simultaneously, the jeans market began to show modest declines in the United States and larger declines in foreign markets. In response, the company reduced the number of its facilities and laid off workers. By 1988, a corporate reorganization focused the company on basic product lines, trimmed the number of marketing divisions from seventeen to five, and eliminated layers of management. As a result of these changes and the market, the company closed twenty-six plants and pared its work force of thirty-eight thousand by 16 percent — an unpleasant decision for an employer long known for benevolence and lifetime employment.

This challenge to company values would soon lead to some deep soul-searching. It would take its first concrete expression in 1987, with the development of the Levi Strauss & Co. Mission and Aspirations Statement, a major initiative to define the shared values that would guide both management and the work force (see Exhibit 9.1). These six Aspirations reflected many of the company's historical traditions and values as well as basic sound management practices. They were a response to the 1980s crisis and an attempt to bring historical values back into alignment with actions. In addition, changes in the marketplace and the work force indicated a need for empowering the work force by pushing responsibility for making decisions closer to those who did the work.

In an interview published in the *Harvard Business Review,* Haas explained the philosophy behind the Aspirations:

> A company's values — what it stands for, what its people believe in — are crucial to its competitive success. Indeed, values drive the business. At Levi Strauss & Co., our Aspirations are our values.
>
> In the past, we always talked about separating the "hard stuff" from the "soft stuff." The soft stuff was the company's commitment to our work force. And the hard stuff was what really mattered: getting pants out the door. What we've learned is that the soft stuff and the hard stuff are becoming increasingly intertwined.
>
> Values are where the hard stuff and the soft stuff come together. Let me give an example: in the new, more dynamic business environment, a

Exhibit 9.1 Levi Strauss & Co. Mission and Aspirations Statement.

LEVI STRAUSS & CO.

MISSION STATEMENT

The mission of Levi Strauss & Co. is to sustain profitable and responsible commercial success by marketing jeans and selected casual apparel under the Levi's® brand.

We must balance goals of superior profitability and return on investment, leadership market positions, and superior products and service. We will conduct our business ethically and demonstrate leadership in satisfying our responsibilities to our communities and to society. Our work environment will be safe and productive and characterized by fair treatment, teamwork, open communications, personal accountability and opportunities for growth and development.

ASPIRATION STATEMENT

We all want a Company that our people are proud of and committed to, where all employees have an opportunity to contribute, learn, grow and advance based on merit, not politics or background. We want our people to feel respected, treated fairly, listened to and involved. Above all, we want satisfaction from accomplishments and friendships, balanced personal and professional lives, and to have fun in our endeavors.

When we describe the kind of LS&CO. we want in the future what we are talking about is building on the foundation we have inherited: affirming the best of our Company's traditions, closing gaps that may exist between principles and practices and updating some of our values to reflect contemporary circumstances.

What Type of Leadership is Necessary to Make our Aspirations a Reality?

New Behaviors: Leadership that exemplifies directness, openness to influence, commitment to the success of others, willingness to acknowledge our own contributions to problems, personal accountability, teamwork and trust. Not only must we model these behaviors but we must coach others to adopt them.

Diversity: Leadership that values a diverse workforce (age, sex, ethnic group, etc.) at all levels of the organization, diversity in experience, and a diversity in perspectives. We have committed to taking full advantage of the rich backgrounds and abilities of all our people and to promote a greater diversity in positions of influence. Differing points of view will be sought; diversity will be valued and honesty rewarded, not suppressed.

Recognition: Leadership that provides greater recognition—both financial and psychic—for individuals and teams that contribute to our success. Recognition must be given to all who contribute: those who create and innovate and also those who continually support the day-to-day business requirements.

Ethical Management Practices: Leadership that epitomizes the stated standards of ethical behavior. We must provide clarity about our expectations and must enforce these standards through the corporation.

Communications: Leadership that is clear about Company, unit, and individual goals and performance. People must know what is expected of them and receive timely, honest feedback on their performance and career aspirations.

Empowerment: Leadership that increases the authority and responsibility of those closest to our products and customers. By actively pushing responsibility, trust and recognition into the organization we can harness and release the capabilities of all our people.

company has to understand the relationship between work and family. It used to be that what happened to our employees when they went home at the end of the day was their business. But today, that worker's sick child is your business, because if they're worrying about their child or calling in sick when they aren't — and probably feeling resentful because they've had to lie — then they aren't going to be productive.

By contrast, if employees aren't worrying about things outside the workplace, if they feel supported — not just financially but "psychically" — then they are going to be more responsive to the needs of customers and of the business. That support needs to come in a whole set of managerial areas: supervisory practices, peer relations, training, work organization, access to information, and the like. We've had to communicate this message to our employees, and an important way to communicate values is through training. We've developed a comprehensive training program that we call the core curriculum. The centerpiece is a week-long course known as "leadership week" that helps managers practice the behavior outlined in our Aspirations statement. We're rolling out a similar program to other employees in the company including plant supervisors and sewing-line instructors.

Our journey is incomplete. But compared with, say, five years ago, there definitely is a change. Suddenly, this $4 billion company feels like an owner-operated company, which is the goal.

The Levi-Strauss & Co. of the future is going to be shaped by our people and their actions, by the questions they ask and the response we give, and by how this feeds into the way we run our business — mixing the soft stuff with the hard stuff.[8]

When Haas and his management team originally set out to integrate the Aspirations into the organization, it was assumed that the formulation of an Aspirations statement combined with a communications effort on senior management's part would be sufficient to bring about a change in the organization. But by mid-1988, it became clear that simply formulating and endorsing a mission statement produced few if any tangible results. That discouragement led to the development of Leadership Week. Sue Thompson, director of Human Resource Development, commented:

> What senior management has learned is that this is not a casual undertaking. This is a major shift in their own education about the process. When the Aspirations came out in August of 1987, Bob Haas and the Executive Management Committee (EMC) probably thought that by having the senior people communicate it back to the divisions, it would just happen. By mid-1988, nothing had happened. Then Bob [Haas] realized the dilemma and got together with human resources to develop a program.
>
> I really don't think the EMC realized how potentially big the Aspirations would be. I don't think they realized the demands that would be placed on them. They face ever-increasing demands. Yet my sense is that the EMC really has a commitment — they understand that they have to "walk the talk" for it to work.

To ground the Aspirations, management realized that the company had to train employees on how to fulfill the Aspirations as well as gain public commitment to the project. In the spring of 1989, the company initiated the Leadership Week program using a company-adapted version of Kouzes and Posner's Leadership Challenge program. This program was envisioned to serve as the primary vehicle for "spreading the word."

As of 1991, some fourteen hundred employees had completed the course. This involvement of the organization reflects the company's commitment to the process. Chairman Haas described the aim of Leadership Week as follows:

> You can't train anybody to do anything that he or she doesn't fundamentally believe in. That's why we've designed Leadership Week to give people an opportunity to reflect on their own values and to allow them to say what they want to get from work. In most cases, people learn that their personal values are aligned with those of the company. Of course, not everybody will buy into it. We've had some very honest discussions where managers say, "Look, I'm 53 years old, I've managed one way all my life and been successful, and now the company wants me to change. I don't know if I can do it."
>
> But two things happen during Leadership Week. Because the groups are small, people build up a support network. They realize that others have the same problem that they have. Suddenly, they don't feel so alone.
>
> Second, the training makes clear what's expected of them and what the consequences of succeeding or failing to adapt will be. It gives people the freedom to opt out. The real success of our core curriculum will be if it convinces some people that our environment is simply not right for them.
>
> We also try to make sure that the core curriculum isn't just some nice experience that stops as soon as people get back to their jobs. For instance, there is a section of Leadership Week called "unanswered questions" where people voice concerns inspired by the course. Our human resources people collect these unanswered questions and report on them every quarter to the Executive Management Committee. Sometimes, these questions can be handled by a particular individual. In other cases, we've set up a companywide task force to

study the issue and come back with suggestions for
changes in the way we do things. This creates a di-
alogue within the company among the people who
have to make things happen.[9] [Copyright © by the
President and Fellows of Harvard College. All
rights reserved.]

It also became apparent that even with the involvement
of employees in Leadership Week this was insufficient to change
the organization. A survey conducted in 1989 of 2,673 individuals at corporate headquarters showed that while employees understood and supported the company's values as stated in the
Aspirations, they did not believe they were being acted out (Levi
Strauss & Co., *NewsWatch*, Nov. 8, 1989, p. 4). Respondents
were relatively certain they supported the Aspirations, but they
felt uncertain about whether others did, especially in terms of
empowerment and diversity in the workplace.

The next step, then, was to look at other organizational
mechanisms to reinforce and reward the practices outlined in
the training program. Several were put into place:

1. communications through company newsletters
2. rewards
3. performance appraisals
4. task forces
5. organizational development consultants
6. gainsharing programs

Through these devices, it was hoped that much of the
newly learned information would be cultivated back on the job.
Newsletters highlighted achievements of work groups in living
the Aspirations. Special recognition rewards were created for
innovation, risk taking, and the achievement of Aspirations. Organizational development consultants assisted the company divisions in implementing many of the Aspirations.

Task forces were formed to address various issues related
to leadership and empowerment. For example, concerns that
invisible barriers to women and minorities were keeping them

from advancing in the organization led to diversity being adopted as one of the six Aspirations. In 1987, members of the company's Executive Management Committee began meeting with groups of fifteen to twenty employees to discuss problems facing minorities within the company. These forums became the catalysts for several important initiatives. Among them were the establishment of four career-development courses, one each for women, blacks, Hispanics, and Asians. In 1989, a three-day course entitled Valuing Diversity was inaugurated; it had been attended by the top 240 managers by the end of 1990.

Experiments are currently being made with gainsharing plans to determine their effectiveness in encouraging greater plant leadership and initiative. In Blue Ridge, Georgia, Levi Strauss established productivity improvement goals at one of its jeans factories, agreeing to share the savings with employees. Formerly the second-best plant in terms of cost of goods produced, by 1990 it became the best by 7 percent.

Most interesting, however, was Levi Strauss's incorporation of leadership development into the company's performance appraisal. Today one-third of the appraisal is based on the demonstration of Aspirational behavior, and 100 percent of an individual's salary increase is tied to the overall performance appraisal. While the concept is novel and potentially quite powerful, one difficulty has surfaced: the deviation around the mean on the leadership dimension is small in reality (implying that people are not seeing or assessing critically the magnitude of differences between individual employees). One would hope, instead, to see considerable deviation. So this section of the appraisal may not be taken as seriously as it needs to be to foster change. However, a senior-level task force is currently considering several potentially dramatic innovations in the overall evaluation and compensation system, which will address such problems as these. An entirely new performance management and pay delivery system has been developed to ensure that the evaluation and reward systems support the Aspirations statement. Most noteworthy is that the process used to develop the system components itself reflected the Aspirations. For example, five task forces were used, which were composed of more than eighty people representing all functions in the company. Broad principles were identified up front, and then the task forces had the freedom to create what they felt was appropriate, as long as the results supported the principles.

What the Levi Strauss & Co. case illustrates is that the process is an ongoing one. There are no simple or quick answers. There has to be considerable experimentation. As a result, a continual and strong commitment from management is crucial to getting through the long transition period. The tendency in many companies is to give up too soon.

When asked what critical lessons have been learned from the experience, Sue Thompson commented:

> The first and most important piece of the process is Senior Management. The initial step into a process like this is a leap of faith. If the CEO is not committed, there is no hope of it succeeding.
>
> Second, LS&Co. had its culture going for it. We are a family-oriented culture — very paternalistic. We care for our people. During the Depression, we went to a two-and-a-half day workweek at our San Francisco plant just to keep people working. When there wasn't enough work, they refinished factory floors. In our case, senior management is positioning the effort as part of our overall business strategy. It was critical to have the EMC's (Executive Management Committee) sponsorship. And to have them teaching and facing course participants. To have them face the angry plant management — it really kept them in touch with reality. In terms of changes I would have made, I would have redirected our resources to work on skills. So when people learned about empowerment, they would have an empowerment skills training component. It's important to be timely. When people are learning about the concepts, that's when they want and need the skills training.

Change is slow. At the home office, there's a critical mass of people, so it feels like things are happening. But in other parts of the company, the same old issues are still there. A lot of cynics. Also there are cultural issues that must be addressed when training the ideas of leadership and Aspirations outside of the headquarters. Material with a cheerleading emphasis or films of Martin Luther King speeches just don't fit over in Europe.

Peter Thigpen, senior vice president of operations, remarked:

The leveraged buyout in 1985 really focused our attention — get that debt down. By 1987, we were starting to breathe. It was like a rejuvenation of our original values. During the early 1980s, it was as if our values and traditions had been suspended. The aspirations were really already there — waiting to be revived. The Aspirations statement allowed us to link responsible commercial success with a way to achieve personal success — integrating both the commercial and personal or societal contribution side. I call it a code of conduct.

We are dealing here with something of great magnitude, and the jury is still out on whether it will succeed. In April and May of 1989, we began our first Leadership Week. We also concluded that it was important that it be taught by the Executive Management Council. We thought that this kind of example of our commitment was crucial. People will believe you if you do it. And one of the ways that people start to believe you is when you show our own [executives'] struggles with implementing the Aspirations. It is important to be very open about your own failures — to make it okay to fail.

One gets a great sense of the starts and stops of these processes, of their difficulty, of their mag-

214 Learning to Lead

nitude, of the down days, of the persistence required. In a way, I think the biggest risk we face
is that we will lose patience.

The real success is that we started it in the
first place.

I think that what we have learned so far is
that it is important to measure progress more tightly
with benchmarks. They [human resources] did a
survey in mid-1989, then later mid-1991. Measure-
ment is key. Once every two years is not enough.

Also, I believe that the element of public
commitment is very important. In Leadership
Week, people commit to acting differently. So it
becomes a way of holding people accountable.

It is also important to emphasize that Leadership Week is not all about leadership. Followership
is equally important. I believe you cannot be a good
leader until you have been a good follower — as a
leader, you have to be able to empathize with your
followers. You can't stand too many leaders in one
organization. So one aspect of Leadership Week
is to encourage good followership. Also, from my
perspective as a manufacturing executive, I feel it
would have been important to have installed the
quality process in the system before the course. It
would have forced employees to empower, communicate, concentrate on the customer beforehand.
The training would have reinforced all of that.

These comments are a powerful reminder that leadership
development is a complicated and time-consuming process. It
requires a very serious commitment in terms of time and resources — much as Plato's program did. There are no quick or
magic solutions; rather it is a never-ending process that demands
continual experimentation and dogged persistence.

To conclude, we might say that the art of leadership development is still very much in its infancy. We are only beginning to understand some of the potential tools that training can

offer us. In addition, organizations must increasingly share the principal responsibility for nurturing leaders. I am convinced that leadership training, for many organizations, is merely a quick-fix answer to say they are concerned about developing leaders, when, in reality, they feel more secure with managers. This attitude will have to disappear if we truly wish to see more leaders in the organizations of the future. A challenge awaits us.

Appendix

The Research

*T*his book's findings are based on two research approaches: participant observation and field interviews. With roots in anthropology and sociology, participant observation essentially involves having the researcher participate in and observe the phenomena to be studied. In this project, either myself or my research assistant actively participated in the training programs as trainees ourselves. We used journals to record program events and personal reactions and observations. In these journals we also recorded impressions of preprogram work, afterprogram experiences, and the personal lessons that we learned.

The second approach, research interviews with fellow participants, was conducted during and after programs. In every program, we actively interviewed participants while the programs were progressing to ascertain their views on program design, effectiveness, and outcomes. Typically, these interviews involved open-ended questions about a particular experience, what participants were learning, or overall impressions of the program. After each program's completion, we followed up with telephone interviews some three to six months later. These interviews averaged thirty minutes in duration and were conducted

216

either by myself or by research assistants trained in interviewing. On occasion, second interviews were conducted with participants who were willing to spend more time sharing their experiences and/or who had had strongly positive or averse experiences. Samples of typical telephone interview questions are listed in Exhibit A.1. By program, we interviewed the following number of participants:

Program	Participants
ARC's VisionQuest	14
Forum's Leadership	8
LeaderLab	26
The Leadership Challenge	30
Leadership Development Program	24
Pecos River LEAD	46

Under ideal circumstances, we would have preferred to have included the subordinates, peers, and superiors of participants in interviews, but time and limited resources precluded this more extensive form of investigation. As well, it would have been useful to have interviewed a larger sample; to have had more time-staggered interviews before, during, and after each program; and to have employed a control group. Again, resource and time constraints precluded these possibilities. As such, it is important to consider this study as exploratory research.

One faces many difficulties in attempting to investigate leadership training with rigor. Because of this, program evaluation has largely been the provenance of company studies rather than academic research. These studies have tended to be conducted quite casually. As researchers Latham and Saari lament: "The typical approach to evaluation of a training program is to review the program with one or two vice-presidents, various managers in the field, and perhaps a group of prospective trainees. If the program "looks good," the company uses it until someone in a position of authority decides that the program has outlived its purpose. All of this is done on the basis of opinion and judgment. In the end, no one really knows whether the training attained the objectives for which it was designed."[1]

One of the principal reasons for this lack of rigor is the difficulty that researchers must face in obtaining accurate measurements of program outcomes and the rigorous control of possible intervening factors. Specifically, how do we isolate the particular experience or event that triggered the learning that a participant experiences? It is virtually impossible in programs as complicated as those examined in this book. Secondly, how do we precisely measure outcomes if we are not clear about the exact criterion we wish to measure? For example, if we wish to measure risk taking or strategic skills, how do we do so in a meaningful way? Both are complex constructs that are extremely difficult to operationalize. Furthermore, how would we ensure that all participants have similar backgrounds, are facing the same life issues, and have similar back-home situations, to be certain that we are comparing "apples with apples"? Clearly, this is not possible in real-life programs such as these.

These are but some of the many difficulties that researchers studying such a complex process as leadership training must face. For this very reason, such studies are rare. All of this is to say that a project like this one can only be seen as a beginning. Its shortcomings will have to be addressed by future studies. Given the critical importance of the subject and the enormous resources expended annually by corporations, we can only hope that such explorations will become more commonplace and more extensive.

Exhibit A.1. Sample Research Interview Questionnaires.

Center for Creative Leadership Program

1.   How did the Center for Creative Leadership program affect you the first few weeks back on the job? (Any particular experiences or stories?) How has the program affected the way you lead or manage today? Any tangible results? Examples?
2.   Have your relationships with your superiors, peers, and/or subordinates been affected? Examples?
3.   Are you in any way different today as a manager or leader? Give examples. Do you feel you are a better leader or manager?
4.   What did you feel were the most effective of the training experiences in terms of having a long-term effect? Why do you feel it worked so well for

Exhibit A.1. Sample Research Interview Questionnaires, Cont'd.

---

you? What were the weak parts of the program? What experiences did you find difficult or impossible to bring back to the office? What experiences had an impact that did not last long?

5. What would you have liked to have seen added to or removed from the program to make it more effective for you?

6. Did the extensive feedback from the course affect your behavior in any way? Do you feel the program changed you, as a person, in a fundamental way? In an incremental way? What would have been the key catalyst? Did you find one form of feedback more effective than another (for example, instrument versus staff feedback, or a particular instrument)? Do you feel sure you can attribute these changes to the program, or did other events in your life effect them?

7. Do you still find the theoretical framework(s) of the course useful and find occasion to refer to it? Which parts are the most memorable and meaningful to you?

8. How important is this type of training for your career? Do you think that experiences like this can make someone into a leader? What is their value in terms of leadership development?

9. What hindered the training experience when you came back to the office? What helped the training experience take hold when you came back? (For example, organizational/boss factors.)

10. Would you consider attending another leadership development program in the future? Why or why not? Do you think training can develop leadership skills?

The Leadership Challenge Workshop

1. How did The Leadership Challenge program affect you the first few weeks back on the job? Has The Leadership Challenge workshop changed you as an individual, manager, or leader? Have your leadership skills been enhanced and if so, how? Examples?

2. Have your relationships with your superiors, peers, and/or subordinates been affected? Examples?

3. What is the most valuable learning experience(s) of The Leadership Challenge program for you and why? Why do you feel it worked so well for you? What were the weak parts of the program? What experiences did you find difficult or impossible to bring back to the office? What experiences had an impact that did not last long?

4. Do you still find the theoretical framework(s) of the course useful and find occasion to refer to it? Which parts are the most memorable and meaningful to you?

5. Have you been able to follow up on the commitments that you made at the workshop? Have you contacted your "buddy" about your mission statement? Why or why not?

6. What have been the most difficult obstacles in your path preventing you from putting into practice some of the things that you would have liked to put into practice?

Exhibit A.1. Sample Research Interview Questionnaires, Cont'd.

---

7. What would you have liked to have seen added to or removed from the program to make it more effective for you?
8. Was the feedback both from your peers and the professionals relevant and pertinent to the program? Did it effect some behavior change?
9. Why do you think that the program worked so well/didn't work so well/didn't work at all for you? Is it due to factors within or outside the program? Examples?
10. Would you consider attending another leadership development program in the future? Why or why not? Do you think training can develop leadership skills?

Notes

Chapter 1

Epigraph: W. Berry, "The One Inch Journey," in *The Unforeseen Wilderness* (New York: Farrar, Straus & Giroux, 1991).

1. R. F. Bales and P. E. Slater, "Role Differentiation in Small Decision-Making Groups," in *Family, Socialization, and Interaction Process*, ed. T. Parson, R. F. Bales, and others (Glencoe, Ill.: Free Press, 1955); D. Cartwright and A. Zander, Eds., *Group Dynamics: Research and Theory* (New York: Harper & Row, 1968); E. A. Fleishman, E. F. Harris, and H. E. Burtt, *Leadership and Supervision in Industry* (Columbus, Ohio: Bureau of Educational Research, Ohio State University, 1955); A. W. Halpin and B. J. Winer, *The Leadership Behavior of the Airplane Commander* (Columbus, Ohio: Ohio State University Research Foundation, 1952); G. A. Yukl, *Leadership in Organizations* (Englewood Cliffs, N.J.: Prentice Hall, 1989).

2. E.J.H. Andriessen and P.J.D. Drenth, "Leadership: Theories and Models," in *Handbook of Work and Organizational Psychology,* ed. P.J.D. Drenth, H. Thierry, and others (New York: Wiley, 1984), 489.

3. R. R. Blake and J. S. Mouton, *The Managerial Grid* (Houston: Gulf Publishing, 1964).

Chapter Two

Epigraph: M. Shelley, *Frankenstein* (New York: Bantam Books, 1981).
1. W. G. Bennis, "Leadership Theory and Administrative Behavior: The Problem of Authority," *Administrative Quarterly 4* (1959): 259–260.
2. W. G. Bennis and B. Nanus, *Leaders: The Strategies of Taking Charge* (San Francisco: HarperCollins, 1985).
3. R. M. Stogdill, *Handbook of Leadership: A Survey of the Literature* (New York: Free Press, 1974).
4. G. A. Yukl, *Leadership in Organizations* (Englewood Cliffs, N.J.: Prentice Hall, 1989), 2.
5. J. P. Kotter, *A Force for Change: How Leadership Differs from Management* (New York: Free Press, 1990), 5.
6. As well, there are cultural variations on leadership that must be recognized outside of North American contexts. For example, Geert Hofstede's study at IBM involving 80,000 employees from sixty-seven countries indicated significant differences by country in terms of individualism and power distance. These factors play themselves out in terms of leadership differences between nations. For more information, see G. Hofstede, *Culture's Consequences* (Beverly Hills, Calif.: Sage Publications, 1980), and "Motivation, Leadership, and Organization: Do American Theories Apply Abroad," *Organizational Dynamics* (Summer 1980): 42–63.
7. T. Bouchard, "All About Twins," *Newsweek,* 23 Nov. 1987, 69.
8. D. Goleman, "Major Personality Study Finds That Traits Are Mostly Inherited." *New York Times,* 1 Dec. 1986, C1.
9. H. Gardner, *The Theory of Multiple Intelligences* (New York: Basic Books, 1985), 35.
10. T. Owen Jacobs and E. Jacques, "Military Executive Leadership," in *Measures of Leadership,* ed. K. Clark and

M. Clark (Greensboro, N.C.: Leadership Library of America, 1990).

11. Gardner, *Theory of Multiple Intelligences,* 239.
12. D. J. Isenberg, "How Senior Managers Think," *Harvard Business Review* (Nov.-Dec. 1984): 81-90.
13. J. W. Gardner, "Leadership Development," *Leadership Paper 17* (June) (Washington, D.C.: Independence Sector, 1987), 10.
14. J. M. Burns, *Leadership* (New York: Harper & Row, 1978), 94-95.
15. Burns, *Leadership,* 113.
16. Burns, *Leadership,* 94-95.
17. Burns, *Leadership,* 117.
18. W. James, *Varieties of Religious Experiences* (New York: Mentor Books, 1958).
19. A. Zaleznik, "Managers and Leaders: Are They Different?" *Harvard Business Review* (May-June 1977): 67-78.
20. A. Zaleznik, "The Leadership Gap," *The Executive 4* (1) (1990): 9.
21. M.F.R. Kets de Vries, "Origins of Charisma: Ties That Bind the Leader and the Led," in *Charismatic Leadership,* ed. J. A. Conger and R. N. Kanungo (San Francisco: Jossey-Bass, 1988).
22. J. M. Burns, *The Lion and the Fox* (New York: Harcourt Brace Jovanovich, 1956), 6-10.
23. Zaleznik, A., "Managers and Leaders."
24. W. M., McCall, M. M., Lombardo, and A. M. Morrison, *The Lessons of Experience* (Lexington, Mass: Lexington Press, 1988), 3-5.
25. Kotter, *A Force for Change.*
26. McCall, Lombardo, and Morrison, *The Lessons of Experience,* 145.
27. R. Boyatzis, "Beyond Competence: The Choice to Be a Leader," paper presented at the Academy of Management Meetings, San Francisco, 1990.
28. J. Loevinger, *Ego Development* (San Francisco: Jossey-Bass, 1980).
29. D. J. Levinson, *The Seasons of a Man's Life* (New York: Knopf, 1978).

30.   R. E. Boyatzis and D. A. Kolb, "Assessing Individuality in Learning: The Learning Skills Profile," *Educational Psychology* 11 (3 & 4) (1991): 279–295.

Chapter Three

Epigraph: Plato, *The Republic,* trans. D. Lee (New York: Penguin Books, 1987), 347–349.
1.   Plato, *The Republic,* 354.
2.   A. P. Carvevale, L. J. Gainer, and A. S. Meltzer, *Workplace Basics* (San Francisco: Jossey-Bass, 1990), 382.
3.   J. F. Bolt, "Tailor Executive Development to Strategy," *Harvard Business Review* (Nov.–Dec. 1985): 168–176.
4.   M. S. Bassin, "Developing Executive Leadership: A General Foods Approach," *Personnel Journal 65* (Sept. 1988): 38–42.
5.   See Chapter 12 of Richard Boyatzis's *The Competent Manager: A Model for Effective Performance* (New York: Wiley, 1982) for a similar and more detailed description of such approaches.

Chapter Four

Epigraph: A. H. Maslow, *Toward a Psychology of Being* (New York: D. Van Nostrand, 1968).
1.   P. Galagan, "Between Two Trapezes," *Training and Development Journal 41* (March 1987): 40–50.
2.   Galagan, "Between," 354–355.
3.   For a full description of one version of the lifeboat exercise, see *The 1990 Annual: Developing Human Resources,* ed. J. W. Pfeiffer (Palo Alto, Calif.: University Associates, 1990).

Chapter Five

Epigraph: C. Fadiman, *The Little, Brown Book of Anecdotes.* (Boston: Little, Brown, 1985).
1.   When I employ the term *conceptual* to describe these programs, I do not mean that they teach only concepts, rather that they are built around a conceptual model which guides

the coursework. For example, in the case of The Leadership Challenge, the practices that constitute the model are research based and behavioral.
2. The Leadership Challenge™, copyright 1987, 1989, 1991. Kouzes Posner International, Inc. All rights reserved. Published by TPG/Learning Systems, A Tom Peters Company.

Chapter Six

Epigraph: Center for Creative Leadership, "Essentials of Constructive Feedback" (Greensboro, N.C., 1988).
1. The LDP development group included Bob Bailey, Dobbin Franklin, Jenny Godwin, Stan Gryskiewicz, Al Scarborough, and Bill Sternberg.
2. D. Campbell, "Inklings," *Issues and Observations* 10 (2) (1990): 11.
3. This exercise is adapted from *Structured Experiences for Human Relations Training,* ed. J. W. Pfeiffer and J. E. Jones, Vol. 11 (Palo Alto, Calif.: University Associates, 1974).
4. These ideas are derived from models developed by Tannenbaum and Schmidt (1958) and Vroom and Yetton (1973), which tie the level of decision-making participation by subordinates to their expertise, ability, and needs for ownership. See R. Tannenbaum and W. H. Schmidt, "How to Choose a Leadership Pattern," *Harvard Business Review* (Mar.–Apr. 1958); and V. H. Vroom and P. W. Yetton, *Leadership and Decision-Making* (Pittsburgh, Pa.: University of Pittsburgh Press, 1973).

Chapter Seven

Epigraph: K. Sekida, *Zen Training* (New York: Weatherhill, 1977).
1. A detailed description of the research and findings appear in "Special Report on Leadership," in *Forum Issues,* Jan. 1990, published by Forum Company, Boston, Mass.
2. The four clusters of practices are presented in this chapter by kind permission of the Forum Company, © 1990.

Chapter Eight

1. L. Wilson "Come to the Ranch and Play the Game," *Training and Development Journal* (Mar. 1987): 49–50.

2. K. Lewin, *Resolving Social Conflict* (New York: Harper & Row, 1948); G. Prince, *The Practice of Creativity* (New York: Collier, 1970); G. Prince, "Putting the Other Half of the Brain to Work," *Training: The Magazine of Human Resource Development,* No. 11, 1978.

3. This is somewhat in contrast to several evaluations conducted by the Center for Creative Leadership on their Leadership Development Program. Specifically, the first formal survey in 1976 of past participants showed that of the respondents (52 percent of total sample), 99 percent indicated using one or more of the Leadership Development Program components, and 90 percent reported using material from four or more components. As well, 69 percent described positive changes in their behavior as a result of staff feedback. The Roger Hull Foundation conducted a longitudinal study of the program and concluded that "although the success reported by each individual varied, it is important to note that an insight was gained or a behavior modified in all participant cases." A 1982 mail survey of participants of fifty-two public Leadership Development Program offerings showed that of the 42 percent who responded, positive behavior change resulting from staff feedback was reported by 87 percent. The Center continues to conduct these evaluations to this day.

4. B. Berelson and G. A. Steiner, *Human Behavior: An Inventory of Scientific Findings* (New York: Harcourt Brace, 1964); W. Byam, D. Adams, and A. Kliggins, "Transfer of Modeling to the Job," *Personnel Psychology,* No. 29, 1976.

5. Berelson and Steiner, *Human Behavior;* J. A. McGeogh and A. L. Irion, *The Psychology of Human Learning* (New York: Longmans, Green, 1952).

6. J. A. Conger, *The Charismatic Leader* (San Francisco: Jossey-Bass, 1989) and F. R. Westley and H. Mintzberg, "Profiles of Strategic Vision: Levesque and Iaccoca," in *Charismatic Leadership,* ed. J. A. Conger and R. N. Kanungo (San Francisco: Jossey-Bass, 1988), 161–212.

Chapter Nine

1. This finding is somewhat in contrast to a 1989 evaluation by the Center for Creative Leadership of its Leadership Development Program goal report system. The Center found that 53 percent of program participants did return their completed goal forms, which covered 1,110 goals. Of these 1,110 goals, 337 had been completed, 693 were still in progress, and 80 had been dropped.
2. R. M. Burnside and V. A. Guthrie, "Developing Leaders for the Twenty-First Century" (Greensboro, N.C.: Center for Creative Leadership, 1991), 36.
3. Burnside and Guthrie, "Developing Leaders," 38–39.
4. Burnside and Guthrie, "Developing Leaders," 41.
5. T. Allbright, "Michigan's Global Leadership Program Looks at 1990," *The Bricker Bulletin,* Princeton, N.J., 1990.
6. The following historical material on GE's Crotonville is from an article by Noel M. Tichy, "GE's Crotonville: A Staging Ground for Corporate Revolution," *The Academy of Management Executives* Vol. III, No. 2 (1989): 99–106 and from J. L. Noel and R. Charan, "Leadership Development at GE's Crotonville," *Human Resources Management,* 27 (4) (1988): 433–447.
7. "Action learning" was a development of Reg Revens, an Englishman, who worked for IMCB, Buckinghamshire, and who developed the technique thirty years ago.
8. R. Howard, "Values Make the Company: An Interview with Robert Haas," *Harvard Business Review* Sept.–Oct. (1990): 133–144.
9. Howard, "Values Make the Company," 139–141.

Appendix

1. G. P. Latham and L. M. Saari, "Application of Social-Learning Theory to Training Supervisors Through Behavioral Modeling," *Journal of Applied Psychology* 64 (3) (1979): 239–246.

Index

229